RECEIVED
22 DEC 1949

HQ 4th Cml
Smoke Generator
Battalion

RECEIVED
22 DEC 1949

HQ 4th Cml
Smoke Generator
Battalion

RECEIVED
22 DEC 1949

HQ 4th Cml
Smoke Generator
Battalion

RECEIVED
22 DEC 1949

HQ 4th Cml
Smoke Generator
Battalion

GYPSY FIDDLER

BY

"PETULENGRO"

EDITED BY

W. B. O'HANLON

FUNK & WAGNALLS COMPANY

NEW YORK

1936

CONTENTS

GYPSY FIDDLER

I

THE CARAVAN

"AMONG the blind, the one-eyed man is King." And, among our fellow-outcasts, we, the fiddlers, were the aristocrats of the roads.

Some of the dignity and privilege of the ancient bards and minstrels hung about us, threadbare and tattered. Our fiddling came down to us from father to son, and the esoteric quality of our trade set us a little apart from the tinkers and basket-makers who were our brethren. Our bodies, unstiffened by manual work, were lithe and quick, and we were the athletes of our kind. Our fingers, nimble from stopping the fiddle-strings, could maneuver a pen across paper, and we were often scribes—for our fellows were illiterate. We were not tied to any one place for even a day. We did not know servility, for we had nothing to sell beyond our fiddling. And so, even among vagabonds, we had more freedom than any.

As well as being "Prastermengros" or fiddlers, my own family belonged to the larger group known, in the Romany tongue, as "Petulengros." The word means traveling farriers and horse-doctors. Thus my particular family, in addition to the knowledge of music, inherited wisdom in the ways of horses and other animals.

Like my sister, my six brothers, my father, and Heaven knows how many other forebears, I was born in a caravan. During my boyhood, the van was my home. I have wandered far from it in my time, but I have always gone back to it.

I cannot account for this queer love of mine. George Borrow's gypsies gloried in their freedom as wanderers—"There's a wind on the heath, brother!"—but I have never found the characteristic very noticeable in real-life gypsies. From my own experience, I can say that the reaction of the typical Romany to a wind on the heath would be much the same as a normal ratepayer's to a draft in the sitting-room.

There is hardly one of us living in van or tent who wouldn't be under a snug suburban roof if he got the chance. The successful among us are. It is only the "submerged tenth" who remain romantically on the heath when the wind is blowing.

Chance decreed that I should be an exception among my fellows as regards temperament: that I should possess the love of road and sky with which popular fancy has invested the gypsy character: that I should sincerely prefer the open heath (with or without wind) to a house with central heating.

My theatrical work makes it necessary that I have more stable headquarters for my orchestra than a caravan could provide, and for this reason I keep a flat in London. But I distrust the place. I distrust my ornaments, my sticks of furniture. They are property, and it has always made me uneasy to possess property. It puts its tentacles round your feet, trying to shackle you to one place. Where there is a hearth and an armchair, there is an awful peril of taking root, against your will. But I thank my stars for the knowledge that my own van is still standing deep in a wood I know of. When the grip of the tentacles becomes too oppressive, I go there.

I never wanted very much to own anything. I have felt hunger and thirst as often as most, but the instinct to hoard against them has never been in me. In my life, I have not worshiped money extravagantly, and certainly not security. To tell the truth, I have never had either quest or creed in life. I have never sought anything with much fervor or constancy except change. I have looked upon the world with a kind of detached interest, and my strongest feelings have come from within myself rather than from outside stimuli. I have felt deeply, but my passions have been of the fundamental kind —joy, despair, anger, indignation, tenderness. At bottom, I am, I think, a primitive type, and certainly I have always found it easy to understand the mind and impulses of primitive peoples—Kaffirs, Brazilian natives, and the like—even Bushmen.

I could not have been more than three when my father began teaching me to play the violin. At the same time, he was instructing one of my brothers in the 'cello; and there must have been strange sounds in the depths of a certain thicket when the two of us scraped away together, practising on instruments as big as our diminutive selves.

At that time, and for some years afterwards, the family van was pitched as a rule in the country lying to the northwest of London, generally at Stanmore or Dollis Hill. In those days, of course, both these places were well away from the town, as the houses of the Metropolis did not extend much beyond Kilburn or Brondesbury in that direction.

I had no great urge to master my music, and no more love than most small boys for practising my instrument. In my boyhood, the "Petulengro" in me was strong, and the "Prastermengro" a very bad second. I had an overwhelming passion for animals of all kinds, and for snakes in particular. There are peculiar folk in the world who are fascinated by snakes, and I am one of these. Indeed, it is more than fascination; it is a kind of affection.

Strange as it may seen, there was a fair number of snakes about the country round Dollis Hill in those days—mostly grass-snakes, it is true, but several belonging to more exotic species. If I had had my choice, I would have spent all my youthful days in hunting for specimens to add to my collection of pets, but my father kept me hard at my fiddle-practise, and, almost against my will, I became a kind of lesser prodigy on the violin.

That extraordinary man, my father, took it upon

himself to be responsible for all our education. His method was somewhat unconventional, but I know of worse systems.

He not only gave us a good grounding in music, but he taught us drawing and painting, and took us on various expeditions to art galleries and museums. A strange wild brood we were, tramping in our alien garments through the aisles of these grave places, a scandal to the curators.

He also taught us some of the great store of knowledge that was in himself: of nature, of horses and dogs, of strange scraps of philosophy and history and physics that he had studied.

The rest of our training was physical. In accordance with the tradition of us fiddlers, he taught us how to box. He also taught us how to swim and ride better than most. And lastly, how to walk. Most of the boys of our class wore hobnails, but he insisted on our wearing the very lightest shoes. Shod in these, he would take us to a nearby railway line, and, stepping on the sleepers, we would walk for miles. The value of this lay in that, by walking on the wood only, we were obliged to take a stride an inch or two longer than the normal. Whether the theory is sound or not, in practise it worked very successfully, for we all turned out famous walkers.

In my own case, there was a curious hiatus in my education. My father did not teach me to read and write. I honestly believe that I had a better all-round knowledge than most children of my age and class, especially as regards certain out-of-the-way and little-known facts, but the extraordinary fact remains that, although my father wrote excellently and read deeply himself, he never passed these accomplishments on to me. Indeed, I was a grown man before I could do either.

When I was about seven, we forsook the van for a period, and moved into a newly built house on the extreme northwest fringe of London. It had a big back-garden, and at the foot of the garden was a railway embankment. Beyond was a broad plain, a wilderness of sorrel and thistles. It was a scraggy ugly stretch of country and, although I and my brothers would play for hours on the railway embankment, performing regularly our walking-exercise between the rails, we disliked the plain and would rarely venture out on it. I can remember distinctly the impression of revulsion it gave me. Even on sunlit afternoons, I seemed to feel a sinister gloom over these tangled fields.

I cannot say whether it was anything psychic in us or not, but the fact remains that our instinct was not at fault. Our aversion was to be justified, and the gloom of the field was to be fulfilled in sinister fashion. It was one of my earliest recollections, and an evil one.

One of my brothers shared a bedroom with me at the back of the house. One summer morning, I woke very early, and could not sleep again. It was still half-dark—that cold uneasy hour of the false dawn. I tossed restlessly in bed for a while, then I got up and went to the window and looked out.

The slope of the garden hid the railway cutting. Beyond stretched the plain, its farther limits lost in the dark mists of half-night, the tangled weeds and bushes nearer at hand standing out, colorless, but sharp-cut in the gray light of daybreak.

Close by the fence bounding the cutting, two dark figures were standing. I could distinguish that they were a man and a woman. The woman hardly moved, but the man's arms were moving as if he were talking excitedly. In that eerie, forlorn hour, shrouded half in darkness, half in light, they looked inexpressibly weird.

Suddenly the man moved, and appeared to clutch at the woman. She seemed to grip his wrists, or he hers, and they struggled, moving their arms and bodies with a sideways sawing motion. With a wrench, they broke apart. For an instant they were static. I was staring, with eyes and mouth wide open, absolutely unmoving. If somebody had crept up behind me at that second and touched my arm, I should have screamed. Then the man sprang forward. His arm performed a wide slashing movement in the air. He seemed to have struck the woman across the face, for she went down like a bag of hay. The man bent over her. . . .

I was released from the spell of horror that had held me. Frightened horribly and trembling, I ran from the window and wakened my brother with whispers.

He came to the window with me and we looked out. The man and woman were both on their feet. She was leaning against the wire fence, and he had an arm round her neck, as if supporting her.

My brother peered at the immobile figures through sleepy eyes. He shrugged.

"If it was a fight, they've made it up again," he said.

We went back to bed, and slept the heavy sleep of children. We did not go out to the garden till late in the morning.

When we did so, the first thing we noticed was a small crowd of people on the other side of the railway cutting, just about the spot where I had seen the two ghostly figures some hours before. By now that scene I had witnessed in the dawn seemed so divorced from reality that I was almost ready to believe I had dreamed it.

Now, however, at the sight of that knot of people, all the instinctive horror I had felt in that sinister dawn returned.

"Come on," said my brother. "Something's happened."

We scrambled over the garden fence, down the bank, across the lines, and up the farther bank. Unobtrusively, we joined the group. The people were standing in a ring, looking down at something on the ground.

It was a woman in a blue dress, a ragged dirty woman with a pale skin. Her throat was slashed across from the angle of one jawbone to the other, an incredibly horrible gash seven inches long and three wide. The neck was half-severed. Her distended eyes stared up at the bright morning sky, dead and lusterless as stones.

My childish mind could not absorb the full horror of that corpse. Blessed numbing unreality held it. I stared steadily at the dead in mingled repulsion and a sort of impersonal interest.

For the first time, a man in the crowd noticed us. "'Ere, this ain't for kids like you," he said. "'Op it!"

He shepherded us away. As we climbed slowly over the fence, I heard him say to someone else:

"We oughter 'a' covered 'er up . . ."

The murderer surrendered to the police a few days later. He and his victim belonged to the tramp class. He had attacked her in a fury because she had bilked him of the change of sixpence he had given her for something. For twopence or threepence he had murdered her. . . .

It was about as ugly and sordid a crime as one could imagine. But, although I had witnessed both the deed and its results, neither left any very deep impression on me. I did not develop any "inhibitions" or "repressions" over it. Perhaps I was too young to be strongly affected. I remembered it, but I had no nightmares about it.

The attitude of other children towards us troubled me more. In those days, the common people had much less education than now, and there was no comparable popular entertainment such as the pictures to broaden their minds. The result was an extraordinary insularity. If they encountered a being that was strange to them, they would jeer and laugh at it—if they were in good humor. If they were in less pleasant mood, they wanted to hurt or maim it.

We, being a strange swarthy folk, were objects of special suspicion. For some reason, which I have never been able to fathom, a conviction arose among the local lads that we were German Jews. Apparently, to be a German Jew was to touch the heights of malevolence and the depths of ignominy. But even if we had been able to prove we were neither Teutonic nor Semitic, it would have made no difference. As creatures who lived and looked differently from themselves, it followed as a matter of course that we should suffer for it. When they met us in numbers, they stoned us.

The local hobbledehoys regarded it as a sacred duty to hunt us down, whenever we ventured from the fields into the streets. Fortunately for us, we were agile in evading the hunters, for it would have been a serious matter for us if we had been tracked down. They commonly wore belts studded with heavy brass knobs, and would have used them on us with as great celerity as their hobnails.

But we had our own ways of defending ourselves.

Things of the wild as we were, we could fashion weapons after the manner of our kind. We had been taught the secret of making a small very neat kind of catapult which could fire stones and even bullets of lead with great force and accuracy. We could also use with some skill that ancient and effective weapon —the sling. We were all fairly expert in the use of these homely arms, and we gave our hunters as good as we got.

I am afraid that, partly from being thus ostracized by the local people, partly from my own inclinations, I was something of a young savage. I remember with great regret my treatment of an unfortunate school-inspector, who made several tentative attempts to interview my parents regarding our non-appearance at school. I followed him along the road for over a mile with my catapult, peppering him from behind a hedgerow with tiny stones. He was a town-bred man, and could never catch me, though he tried hard enough. He never even saw me.

I think I broke that school-inspector's spirit. Each time he made the attempt to reach our house, I drove him back along the road he had come. In the end he gave it up.

By now, I was already a professional musician. At the age of seven, I had been entered by my father for a junior competition in violin-playing. I played after two other rather inexpert children had done their worst, and then I had a marvelous stroke of luck. An epidemic of huff broke out among the rest of the competitors, who declared, sullenly or in tears according to their natures, that they didn't want to play. Neither judges nor fond parents could make them change their minds; and I was awarded the first prize.

Thereafter, from time to time, I got odd engagements. For my sins, I was dressed up to play my solos in a velvet suit with lace collar and cuffs, silk stockings and a feathered hat. In retrospect, taking into account the ungodly spectacle I must have presented, I can understand and almost sympathize with the animosity of the hobbledehoys. If they wanted to throw stones at children dressed after the fashion of van-dwellers, what must they have wanted to do to a small gypsy boy garnished like a Van Dyck portrait!

One of the very first of these early engagements was a very grand affair. I was engaged to play the violin in a juvenile trio, the others being my sister playing the viola, and one of my brothers playing the 'cello. The occasion was a dinner-party at the house of Lady Hobart-Hampden, whose husband was Viceroy of India.

Strange as it may seem, my grandmother was on very friendly terms with Lady Hobart-Hampden. I think the old lady had read her fortune some years before, and one of her long shots in prophecy had come off. It was through my grandmother that we were asked to play.

Picture us three young savages stationed on the staircase of the big house in Cornwall Gardens, Kensington. We had taken up our places there until the guests were finished eating (we were not to play till after the dinner), because it formed a convenient base from which to make quick sallies to steal pieces of food from the plates the footmen were carrying into the dining-room.

We were having the time of our lives escaping from the burdened servants with our tit-bits, and eating them at the head of the stair, until one young footman managed to spoil our childish fun. He was too quick for my sister during one of her lightning forays and grabbed her by the wrist.

"Got you!" he said, and followed it up with a stream of unfootmanly language in a fierce undertone.

My brother and I came dashing to the rescue. But the other member of the family needed no help. She bit the footman on the hand and held on with her teeth.

He tried to shake her off, but she hung on like a terrier. His face was twisted with pain. He wanted to howl, but he was just outside the dining-room door. The dish he carried in his other hand tilted alarmingly. He was trying both to steady the dish and shake off my sister. He managed the latter.

The dish smashed against the wall and spewed its contents in an unsightly blotch over the wallpaper and carpet.

Lady Hobart-Hampden could not have missed hearing the clatter from within the room. In a second or two, she was out in the hall to investigate.

"What's wrong?" she asked the footman.

He was looking like a man who welcomes all the trials he has to bear for the sake of showing how tremendous is his patience.

"She was takin' food off the plate an' I caught 'er," he said. "Then she bit me like a little—dog. After that, I dropped the plate."

Lady Hobart-Hampden turned to my sister with a sort of humorous, defeated expression. The perpetrator of the outrage was looking a perfect picture of charming childish wilfulness.

"I can see that if you wait out here much longer, we shan't have any food—or footmen—left," said our hostess. "I suppose there's nothing for it but to have you in to play at once."

Shouldering our instruments, we tramped into the dining-room. The guests turned to stare at us. We were so small that our chins were barely on a level with the table-top.

"These are the *artistes*," announced Lady Hobart-Hampden. "They seem to have eaten most of our dinner and scandalized the servants, so I thought it perilous to keep them out any longer."

"They look sweet," said a lady. And the curious thing is that I believe we did.

"Now, children," said the Viceroy pleasantly, "I hope you're going to play very nicely for us."

My sister glared at him from under her eyebrows. She had got away with so much that evening that she was a bit above herself.

"I'm not going to play nicely. I'm not going to play for *you* at all!" she declared.

"Oh, dear!" said the Viceroy, assuming an expression of pitiful disappointment.

"But you're not going to play for him altogether," said one of the guests. "You're going to play for all of us."

"I'm not so sure about that," the viola of our trio retorted. "There's a lot of you I don't want to play for."

There was a roar of laughter, then the Viceroy said:

"Suppose you tell us whom—besides myself—you disapprove of, and we'll make ourselves scarce?"

"All right," our viola agreed, unperturbed. "Well, there's you, for a start."

"If I hid myself under the table, would that do?" His Excellency suggested diffidently. "You can see the tablecloth nearly touches the floor. I'm sure we'd be sufficiently out of your way."

My sister considered the point gravely.

"That'll do," she said at last.

And thereupon His Excellency, the Viceroy of India, to the accompaniment of loud cheers from his guests, ducked down and crawled under the table-cloth with as great *savoir faire* as if he were accustomed to perform the operation every day as part of his official duties.

Then my sister went about among the other ladies and gentlemen indicating with the aid of a merciless forefinger which of them had fallen under the ban of her displeasure. They took it extraordinarily well, and, looking back, our own behavior seems worse in contrast. We must have been *enfants terribles* of the most poisonous description. It makes me hot under the collar now to think of it.

When about a dozen distinguished ladies and gentlemen had crawled under the table, my sister announced that we were ready to entertain the favored remainder. We took our instruments from their cases, and, with great composure, began to play.

As we warmed up to it, those who had been banished beneath the table began to creep out one at a time and slip back into their chairs. My sister by then was properly into her stride with the viola, however, and was gracious enough to forget about refusing to allow them to be among her audience.

As may be imagined, it was a curious evening for all of us. Some of the guests must have felt horribly uncomfortable, and must have wanted to strangle us there and then. But, to their eternal credit, if they did feel murderous, they allowed nothing but gaiety to show in their demeanor. They cheered us mightily, and I imagine that we acquitted ourselves very well, as His Excellency sent my sister a very beautiful doll a few days later. If a sense of humor is of any value in administering an Empire, I am sure that our host of that evening must have been a more than usually successful Viceroy.

By the time I was nine, I was making enough money by odd engagements to pay for my keep and buy my own clothes, and it was at that age that I got my first permanent job. This was in the orchestra at the old St. James's Hall, which was on the site now occupied by the Piccadilly Hotel. I played there on Saturday and Sunday nights. On the Saturdays we gave popular concerts, for which old Heath Mills, our conductor, used to pay me 2s. 6d. On the Sundays the Hall was used for services of the West London Mission, the chief attraction being that typical Welsh evangelist, Hugh Price Hughes. For playing on Sundays, I received only 2s., presumably on the assumption that we got the odd sixpennyworth of value out of listening to the famous preacher.

I think ours must have been quite the worst orchestra in London. There were about seventy of us, mostly amateurs, with a small stiffening of professionals. I have always had the greatest sympathy with people who play musical instruments for the love of the thing, but this particular collection of amateurs was about as cracked a lot as you could have found.

Sixty or seventy normal level-headed men and women would meet in the band-room, apparently quite sane and respectable. But sixty or seventy

raving lunatics would emerge on to the concert platform united by a common resolution to scratch and
scrape louder, faster and higher than their neighbors. I think that the unholy uproar of a band of
tortured malevolent fiends in hell would sound very
much like that orchestra.

They would discuss their achievements passionately in the band-room. Their test-piece appeared
to be Paganini's "Moto Perpetuo," and evidently
they would spend their leisure hours in playing the
poor tormented melody at top-speed, with a friend
timing them on a stop-watch. I noticed that they
would boast about their prowess in just the same
way that fishermen are supposed to do, and a violinist who could bring witnesses—which he would and
did—to prove that he had sawed his way through
the said "Moto Perpetuo" in three minutes, would
stand for a while on the same pinnacle of eminence
among his fellow amateurs as might the man among
anglers who has caught a three-foot pike with darn-
ing-wool and a bent nail.

During these last two years we had still been living in the house by the railway embankment. It was
a fairly large house, but curious events were at work
to make it very cramped indeed. My father had
been contentedly busy for some time designing patterns for wallpapers and decorated glass; and then
a well-meaning but misguided friend presented him
with a book called *Amateur Work*. My father's in-
ventive urge could not resist the allurements of that

book. Within a week or so of receiving it, he was stuck all over with glue and bits of paper and wood. He had resolved to build a home-made organ, and no pigmy organ at that. It was to be on a Gargantuan scale, and he meant it to rival, if not excel, the organ in the Town Hall at Sydney (at that time, the biggest in the world!).

Like a giant fungus, the organ grew. Some of its cardboard pipes were big enough in sections to completely fill a room each. My father would work away in one room until he had filled it, then move into another. Presently the monstrous growth of pasteboard and wood filled the whole house.

At last the great project was abandoned. A warehouse (or perhaps two warehouses) would have been needed in which to finish off the building. The completed parts of the organ made the most famous bonfire of all my childhood. We did not regret its going, and yet, when it *had* gone, the house looked bare and unfamiliar. Shortly afterwards we took to the road again, and none of us was sorry.

II

THE FAIR-GROUND

THE personality of my father was the dominating influence upon my early years. He was both an athlete and a musician, a man of powerful esthetic and intellectual urges. Other van-folk, even people much older than himself, regarded him as something of a sage, and would ask him to settle their difficulties and disputes, which he would do somewhat after the manner of King Solomon.

Behind him was immense experience. He had been earning his own living since he was eight years old. In those far-off days—and in my own time—there were, of course, no dance halls or orchestras in cafés and cinemas. Consequently, unless a musician was lucky enough to hold a position at Court, or in an opera house, or something of the kind, he wandered about the country playing at fairs, village dances and weddings, and such-like, often eking out a very uncertain living by performing other tasks. Thus my grandfather, although he ended his career in the orchestra of the Opera at Drury Lane—he did, in fact, actually drop dead while playing in the orchestra-well of that theater —had in his earlier years supplemented his income by working as a traveling farrier, a jockey, an un-qualified veterinary surgeon, and a boxer.

My father remembers, as a child, meeting his re-doubtable parent outside Drury Lane after the Opera and going together to the Coach and Horses in St. Martin's Lane, or perhaps the Mitre. Big Ben Caunt, one-time champion of England and celebrated in the history of the ring for his series of fights with the ferocious Bendigo, kept the Coach and Horses; and Nat Langham, also an ex-cham-pion and one of the few boxers to beat the great Tom Sayers, kept the Mitre. In one or other of these taverns, in a back room, thick with tobacco smoke and the fumes of brandy, my grandfather would engage in bloody fight with some other mu-sician from the Opera, for the diversion of a select number of sporting men—and all for a shilling or two, or a few pots of ale. The fiddlers of those days were a hardy crew!

My father's chief accomplishment, on the other hand, was in a gentler sphere. He became very tal-ented as an artist, and as such has painted many portraits and landscapes. Only five or six years ago, some lettering of his which he exhibited at South Kensington was attributed by the famous art jour-nal, the *Studio,* to Mr. Eric Gill, an error which had to be acknowledged in the next issue of the paper.

In his early years, however, he was obliged to make his talent pay chiefly by painting inn-signs, and in addition he was ready to take on all comers as a professional wrestler and walker. In connection with the latter, I remember riding on a four-in-hand driven by a well-known sporting gentleman which accompanied Dad on a walk he did from London to Colchester and back in twenty-four hours.

During his youthful wanderings about East Anglia he was continually encountering another young man, rather older than himself, who was his great rival as a fiddler at the various fairs and weddings at which he performed. The rival musician, who was a Norfolk gypsy like himself, had a preference for holding his instrument between his knees, as one would a 'cello, when he played. For all that, he had great talent, and he would confide his ambitions to my father. He was a very good boxer, but he had little taste for fighting, being indeed of rather a nervous disposition, but all his dreams were concentrated upon some day becoming a famous violinist.

The nervous young man did become famous, but it was not the musical fame he sought so passionately. Although only about eleven stone, he became the greatest boxer of his time—and, in the opinion of many competent judges, the greatest of all time. His name was Jem Mace.

When he was about seventeen, someone who had taken an interest in my father's ability to write and paint, paid his fare up to London to interview a gentleman who was looking for a companion-secretary. This person, a famous explorer, was about to set off on an expedition to Africa, and wanted someone able to make a pictorial record of any new tribes or animals he might discover.

The interview was arranged to take place at the office of a Mr. C. J. Allen, a solicitor, in Waterloo Place. My father was waiting alone in the outer office, when a very imposing gentleman marched in.

"Do you know if Mr. Allen is in, my man?" he asked.

"No, I don't, pal," answered my father.

The imposing gentleman went red in the face.

"Damn your impudence!" he bellowed. "Do you know who I am?"

"I couldn't say," said my father. "But I suppose you're a cove as can tool a gry and draw a patteran if needs be, and that you're after the same job as I am."

"So that's it, is it?" said the newcomer grimly. "Right, I'll fight you for the job. The loser clears out."

At the same time, he clipped my father under the jaw and grabbed him round the waist. Within about thirty seconds, he was lying flat on his back with my father on top of him.

Hardly had the pair crashed to the floor, when the door of the inner office was flung open, and Mr. Allen, attracted by the sounds of the struggle, came out. When he saw what had happened, his eyes bulged wildly.

"For Heaven's sake get up!" shouted the solicitor.

My father rose self-containedly from his defeated opponent.

"What do you mean by brawling in my office!" the lawyer demanded furiously.

"This chap started it," my father explained. "He hit me on the jaw, so I put him on the carpet."

"Man!" said Mr. Allen in a strangled voice. "Don't you know who this is? It's Sir Charles Legard. It's the gentleman who was going to interview you about going abroad with him!"

He turned apologetically to the explorer.

"Sir Charles, I needn't say how sorry I am—"

The great man, who was dusting himself complacently, held up a hand and cut him short.

"Quite true, you needn't say anything. I enjoyed the little scrap immensely. I should really apologize to you for making such a noise. The young fellow's quite right. I did start it."

He turned to my father.

"You're a handy enough youngster, but I'm afraid you wouldn't suit me. You lost your temper, I noticed, and one man with a temper is enough on a trip of exploration."

Thereupon, he gave his victor a sovereign to compensate him for his outlay on the journey up to London, and begged Mr. Allen to find some other work for him.

Not without some very understandable reluctance, Mr. Allen agreed. As it transpired, however, his doubts were ill-founded, as my faher turned out to be very useful in writing beautiful script and Old English lettering. Not long afterwards, he became clerk to Mr. W. H. Holl at 5, Paper Buildings, Temple—with whom at the time young Edward, afterwards Earl—Grey was reading.

For several years, before returning to his fiddle and the road again, my father remained in this berth, and in the sober atmosphere of the Temple found plenty of time and opportunity to develop his natural taste for study and art.

The old man—and my mother, too—is still alive. Although he is a good ninety, his figure is as slim as a youngster's, and he can walk as briskly as most men of thirty. He has forsaken the van for good, and lives in a large house, furnished rather expensively and in excellent taste, in a highly respectable London suburb. But, by preference, he talks the jargon of the road, and eats off newspapers in the kitchen when he really wants to enjoy a meal—it is more like the van-life he knows best. An evening spent in his house is unique. He might well forget his table manners and use his fingers for a fork, or dip his bread in vinegar. He might be discussing some tinker-rogue of the old time in the language of the hedgerows, or he might be talking about Lessing, or psychoanalysis, or Neo-post-impressionism—with knowledge and no errors in syntax.

Only recently, he made himself responsible for the redecoration of a Baptist church. The entire interior of the church was to be restored, and an architect submitted plans for doing it. My father did not care for the designs, however, and drew up some of his own, which were accepted. These were for all the woodwork, including new pews, pulpit, choir-stalls and organ-base, and all other decoration.

His designs for glassware, as well as specimens of his lettering, have been exhibited at South Kensington, and he has, among other large jobs, done all the glasswork for Harrod's, and the barrel-roof for Dickins and Jones. I believe he still harbors ambitions to have a landscape hung "on the line" at Burlington House.

*   *   *

One day I was sitting outside the van engaged in feeding a ring-snake I had caught. That is to say that I was forcibly stuffing small frogs into him. You must know that snakes, when first in captivity, almost invariably refuse food, and will die unless one makes them eat.

I heard a noise between a cough and a snort, and, looking up, I was confronted with a fair vision in a great poke-bonnet around which was a red band with a design of yellow flames as a badge. She was a very young woman, fair, and beautiful beyond the ordinary. At the moment, however, her strong handsome features were overcast by an expression of such fury, indignation and undisguised dislike that I was reminded in a flash of a picture by G. F. Watts that I had recently seen, the title of which was "Time, Death, and Judgment."

"How can you do such a wicked thing!" she demanded. "Have you no idea, boy, that it's a sin to inflict cruelty on God's creatures!"

I gaped at her. As this was my usual method of feeding my pet snakes, I was astonished by her question, and she would have received a rude answer from me, had I not been too taken aback to find my tongue. Before I could do so, she had swept up the steps of the van, knocked peremptorily on the door, flung it open and disappeared inside.

Piqued by the denunciation I had received, yet oddly impressed by the sincerity and force with which it had been delivered, I withdrew my beloved reptiles to a discreet distance from the van until such time as our unknown visitor left.

When she had done so, I returned and, climbing into the van, asked my father who she was.

"The name of that lady is Miss Eva Booth. You'll go far before you see another like her. Through her, I've found salvation for my sins. Through her, I'll be washed white as snow in the Blood of the Lamb."

Such was my introduction to Evangeline Booth, the present Generalissimo of the Salvation Army. Afterwards I was to find out what drive, gusto, shrewdness and tenacity were in her unique make-up

—and how much humor, a quality sadly lacking in all too many of her co-religionists.

This, too, was my first intimation of my father's succumbing to the infection of religious fervor, a circumstance which, I am afraid, lowered his prestige somewhat in my boyish eyes. I think I had the feeling in my inarticulate mind that his being carried away by mass-emotionalism was a denial of all that was logical and intellectual in him.

In those days Salvationism was much more an affair of hell-fire and hysteria and gnashing of teeth than it is today. The devotees were not treated with the tolerance they are today, but were subjected to fierce ridicule, and it was a favorite pastime of bands of roughs to break up their meetings. As may be imagined, nobody but the most rapt believers took part in these meetings, and, in tough districts of London, I have seen men and women on their knees on the busy pavements, beating their foreheads against the paving stones in an ecstasy of religious fervor, with a ring of roughs round them keeping up a ferocious drunken roaring and howling like a pack of wolves.

It was common for these roughs to commit physical violence on the Salvationists, and for the latter to offer no resistance, but to offer up prayers instead for the misguided sinners whose boots were kicking and fists beating them. There were, however, some less patient spirits among them, men such as my father who could use their hands and were not so swamped in mass-hysteria that they would forbear to do so if provocation became too great. Indeed my father, with a few more of his type, formed a kind of unofficial bodyguard who could generally give a good deal better than they got when it came to a scrap, and I believe that bodyguards such as this had a greater influence in gaining a measure of toleration for the Soldiers of Salvation than much of the hell-fire preaching.

One night, prompted by curiosity as to my father's latest enthusiasm, I followed his corps of the Army to a meeting it was holding in the Edgware Road, at that time the spine of one of the wildest and most unpleasant parts of England.

The faithful were standing in the familiar circle, listening intently to a short stout man testifying exultantly to his salvation. At intervals, one of the circle would bark out a sudden "Hallelujah!" then relapse into silence again. On the outskirts of the circle, a gang of typical local roughs were hooting and cat-calling, pushing and jostling the worshipers on the fringe of the circle, who would stumble forward a foot or two, recover, and stand meekly quiescent again just as if they had not noticed the violent shove they had received.

One of the tormentors in particular was making a nuisance of himself. He seemed to be drunker than most of his friends and kept up an unceasing animal roaring. Suddenly he blundered into the center of the circle. He went reeling about in the clearer space glaring about him stupidly. Seeing a big brass trumpet standing on the ground, he kicked it over with a great clatter. His friends cheered encouragement and jostled the Salvationists beside them still more violently.

I could see my father standing with some other men I knew by sight. I could tell by his set face and the sidelong look in his eyes that he was holding himself in check with difficulty.

The drunk, urged to more destructiveness, ground his heavy boots on a cornet, crushing it almost flat. The small stout man, with his eyes closed, went on with his testimony in a droning monotone, oblivious of all the interruptions. My father started forward, and with him the half-dozen less meek spirits whom I had already recognized. They began to hustle the drunken man out of the ring.

The action was the signal for a wild roar from the man's companions. They burst in a body through the ring in a rush to rescue their friend. In a second there was a wild scuffle, fists and boots flying.

I saw Eva Booth, undaunted, her chin up, making for the center of the disturbance. I heard her voice clear above the clamor:

"There'll be no fighting here!"

There was authority in that cry, even though the order expressed did not take into account the fact that the fighters were already hard at it, rolling on the ground, banging each other's heads against the paving stones, pounding at each other's faces. It was no wonder the command had small effect.

One of the roughs, blundering backwards out of the *mêlée,* cannoned into her. Without a moment's hesitation, he swung his arm and landed her a heavy blow on the jaw.

I cannot say whether or not he was so dazed that he did not realize that it was a woman he was striking, but in any case it was a knock-out blow. Miss Booth went over like a ninepin and lay flat on her back.

In the meantime, the fight had spread outward from its core. All the toughs within hearing distance, overjoyed to find the ice broken, hurried on to the scene and began laying about them. The fat man still droned out his testimony, though the swaying fortunes of the fight were jostling him all over the roadway. Men were going down all over the place, and the women were being knocked down, too, their poke-bonnets rolling like skittles. Instruments were being stamped on, smashed, used as weapons, flung recklessly in the air.

A sudden cry went up:

"The p'lice—!"

The roughs began to run. One of them paused long enough to smash the stout testifier in the face, then took to his heels with the rest. The police arrived. Miss Booth was only just coming round.

I had no illusions about looking any less of a hard case than the ugly characters who had started

the fracas, and not wishing to be mistaken for one
of them I slipped up a convenient side street and
made for a healthier neighborhood as fast as I could
move.

*　　*　　*

For drunkenness, brawls, fights and riots, com-
mend me to that lively district about the Edgware
Road as it was at that period.　Close by the canal
was a big fair-ground, and I spent a large slice of
my adolescence about it.　I think that I must have
been rather more objectionable than are most boys
at that unfortunate age.　By then I was already a
veteran fiddler, but I had long since stopped wearing that horrible suit of lace and velvet, and, from
being the sworn enemy of the young toughs of the
district, I had attained to the status of ring-leader
in their self-conscious villainies.

Picture me at that time as an illiterate, unwashed
young lout, rather more noisy and quarrelsome than
the other louts in whose packs I ran.　My staple
means of livelihood depended on a game called
"Kiss-in-the-ring" which seemed to be immensely
popular at fairs all over England at the time.　If I
remember rightly it was played something like this:
a ring of young men and girls would dance hand
in hand in a circle with one—say a girl—in the
center, who would touch the youth of her choice,
then run; whereupon he would catch her and kiss
her.　Then the youth would be in the middle and
would touch the girl he wanted to kiss, after the

dancing had started again, and so on. It was an incredibly stupid game, the obvious attraction of which lay in the opportunities it offered for expressing the juvenile conception of sex. But how they loved it—and the players were not confined to juveniles!

The usual procedure was for me to put a hat down and wait for the players to collect. As they did so, they would each drop a penny in the hat. When I judged that enough coppers had been collected to make it worth the playing, I would start up my fiddling, and the game would begin.

Every time it was played, various little currents of coquetry and jealousy would be started, and it was not unusual for it to end in a communal brawl. Very often drunken men would pursue girls who had taken their fancy with too much ardor, rousing the anger of the girls' swains, and there was nearly always a fight or two.

It occasionally happened that the players were keener on having their game than in becoming spectators to impromptu fights, and then the one or two men who had started the row would attract the united impatience of the others. In such cases, the crowd was ruthless. The disturbers of the peace would be flung into the all-too-convenient canal, and the game would be re-started.

I, as fiddler, was by no means shut out from this brawling. On one occasion, a young girl marked me out for her temporary swain by tapping me on the shoulder. I kissed her heartily, and had just released her when my shoulder was tapped again, this time in much more aggressive fashion. It was a burly frowning youngster of about eighteen.

" 'Ere, cocky, you stick to your fiddlin', see? That's my gel."

I swore at him and he snarled back at me. I saw what was coming, and, remembering a precept of my father's about "getting in the first blow," I let him have one flush on the nose. The crowd happened to be in a mood for blood and so, instead of chucking us both into the canal as they might have done, they promptly formed a ring and waited for the fight to start.

He was up again right away and came at me with his arms flailing. He was stronger and heavier than I was, but not so active. I was only about fourteen, but I knew a lot more about scrapping. Also, he had been drinking beer and his wind was not as sound as it might have been.

The fight lasted for thirty rounds (the rounds being determined by the number of falls, after the model of the old prize-ring). I retreated and retreated. Throughout these thirty rounds, I don't think I did anything else. I knew I should be murdered if he got at close quarters, so, skipping backwards industriously, I kept my left out and poked him in the face with it.

The crowd were not getting much of a show, but things were going very well for me. I could see my antagonist getting breathless. Then he ran me to earth. In one place the ring of spectators was imperfect and formed a shallow angle. He hemmed me in this angle, and I could not get out. He got an arm round my neck and pounded my face with his free fist, this "head in chancery" hold being apparently quite fair according to the peculiar rules then existent.

I had no intention of taking such a drubbing as was being given me. I knew the secret of several useful wrestling maneuvers, and I brought one into play. I flung him over my head and, as he dropped, completely winded, on his back, I dropped heavily on top of him.

But evidently the lock I had used was a flagrant violation of the curious rules which allowed the "head in chancery" hold. It was not fair to introduce wrestling variations into boxing. The crowd, egged on by some friends of my opponent, howled angrily at me. One or two broke the ring and made for me.

It was plainly no time for argument. Some people well-disposed to me as the smaller fighter made a gap for me and I was through it in a flash.

For three hours I was hunted by a howling mob over a space of ten acres. Thank Heaven, I could run, for in that moment their ancient antipathy had been aroused, they remembered that I was of a strange folk, and were shouting after me the old slogan of "German Jew!" I wonder what they would have done if they had caught me. . . .

For a week or two after that I kept clear of that particular fair-ground. Then, after the crowd had flung one fiddler into the canal for poor playing and beaten the senses out of another for a more disreputable offense, I ventured back, and they were glad to have me.

One evening I was loafing among the vans, when the word went round that a crowd of young toffs from a school lying slightly to the northwest had invaded the district and were making merry in the fair-ground. The schoolboys were unpopular because they had broken some windows in the neighborhood of the canal, and it was agreed that a force must be raised to drive them into their own part of the town.

We marshaled an "army" of unpleasant-looking customers—mostly young loafers about the fair-ground and youths belonging to the families of the bargees on the canal. Among us marched a number of young girls who were just as hardy—and for the most part just as ill-looking—as the males.

Armed with sticks, we sallied into the fair-ground and hurled volley after volley of stones at the invaders. Soon we had them retreating. For the most part, I think the schoolboys realized that they were out of their element and had only ventured into the district in a spirit of bravado. We cleared

them quickly from the fair-ground, driving them
on to the canal bank.

In this stone throwing I was very expert, being
able to throw with both hands with almost equal
accuracy—another trick my early training had
taught me—and my companions were also accustomed to this kind of fighting. The schoolboys, on
the other hand, were very poor at it, and we had a
great advantage.

On the canal bank they made a great stand, however. Among them was notable a very handsome
youth with a pale face and auburn hair, who was
plainly their leader. Thanks chiefly to his efforts,
they kept us at bay for a while, even when we came
to closer quarters and began using our sticks. We
drew off for a bit and began raining stones on them
again, and at this point I flung one with such success—I was low enough to think it such at the time
—that it struck the auburn-haired leader on the
temple and stunned him.

At the same moment we charged. The schoolboys, heavily outnumbered and now leaderless,
broke and fled. We gave chase long enough to be
sure that there was no danger of a rally and counter-
attack, then we paused in our triumph. One casualty still lay on the field of battle—the stricken
leader of the schoolboys. We looked at him with
the eyes of young wolves, and sideways at one another in wary suspicion. Then in a crowd we
rushed at him to pick his pockets. We crowded

round him, arguing and fighting over what spoils there might be and how they should be divided. I remember that a pair of fancy stockings the casualty was wearing with his knickerbocker suit—the kind commonly worn nowadays with a golf suit—excited our cupidity particularly.

Somebody, impatient of so much talk, had already wrenched off one of the fallen boy's shoes and was in the act of stripping off one of the coveted stockings, when he was pushed violently away. The author of the push was one Bridget, a bargee's daughter, and one of the wildest and roughest of our company. In language such as would not have shamed the bargee, her father, she told us the kind of unclean, aborted things we were, and how the forebears from which we were sprung were a long pageant of reptilian unspeakableness.

She cowed the ghouls. Her more powerful personality was more than a match for their lesser hardihood. She stood over the boy's body and dared anybody to touch him. Before the unrelenting flow of her amazing vocabulary, they slunk away, growling with the invariable sullenness of vicious weak things.

I like to think that I had some redeeming qualities at that age. At least I had not been among the ghouls who had advanced to strip the fallen, and now, along with one or two more, I answered to Bridget's command. We lifted the boy and carried him aboard her father's barge.

Bridget and her mother bathed his head and presently he came round. He looked about him.

"Who hit me?" he demanded.

"I did," I said surlily.

"What with?"

"A stone."

"That's a dirty sort of way to fight!" he declared. "I'll pay you for that."

"Want to fight, do you?" I asked aggressively.

"Now, if you like!" he answered, struggling to sit up.

"Quiet, you!" Bridget snapped at me.

"You've had enough fightin' for today," said her mother to the other boy.

Between them, they smoothed us down.

We all stayed on the barge for quite a time that evening. The strange boy, seen at close quarters, was even better looking than he had appeared at a distance. He told us that his first name was Harley. His father was a Harley Street doctor, and had named him after that famous thoroughfare. Bridget kept her eyes on him continually, as if fascinated.

The next night he was back on the fair-ground, this time alone. He seemed to be quite fearless. He recognized me, and we talked. After that, he was always there or thereabouts. Inevitably, he became the leader of us roughs, for he was wilder and more daring than any of us. He became my friend, and one of the best I have ever had.

Among us, I think, his reckless, lawless spirit was in its element. He would perform the wildest actions with a cool insolence which none of us could imitate. With his beautiful hair, brilliant eyes and white delicate face, he could do what he liked with the girls and their mothers. He used to give a call which acted much after the fashion of the pipes of the Pied Piper. When he gave this call, the windows of houses would go up immediately and girls' heads would pop out, while on the canal the bargees' daughters would hurry on deck.

One day, he said to me coolly:

"I've been caught out once too often at school. I'm going to be expelled."

"Are you sure?" I asked.

"It's an absolute certainty," he answered.

And so, apparently, it was. They must have expelled him. If they did, they had good reason. In any case, I lost my friend. He never came back to the fair-ground, and I never saw him again. I wonder what happened to him. . . .

III

THE BATTLE OF THE CLIFFS

At fifteen I looked on myself, with a good deal of smugness, as a veteran fiddler. At that age a letter reached me in the van which made me still more self-satisfied. I could not read the letter, but my father deciphered it for me. It was headed in highly ornamental characters, *"The Isle of Wight Symphony Orchestra. Manager: Weldon Russell,"* and it was signed by that lofty personage Weldon Russell himself. It offered me an engagement to play first violin in the orchestra and summoned me to join it immediately at Shanklin. I noticed with respect that Mr. Russell was a gentleman of too much delicacy to mention anything so vulgar as money.

I wasted no time in going to Shanklin, and made straight for the Concert Hall; but there I could find no sign of the important organization I was to join, nor anywhere else in the town. I thought it impossible that, if an Isle of Wight Symphony Orchestra really did exist, nobody in Shanklin could know about it, and resigned myself to the belief that the letter had been a hoax. Philosophically, I shouldered my fiddle-case and wandered down towards the sea.

Wandering along the cliffs, I presently came to a stretch of pleasant green turf which, from a distance, I could see to be crowded with people.

As I drew nearer, I saw that two bands were playing on the green space, standing a few yards apart from each other, and at the same moment my ears were assailed by the most fiendish cacophony that ever rasped the nerves of a musician. The bands were playing different tunes!

One was clearly the town band, for they were dressed in gorgeous Ruritanian costumes. The other composed a group of about ten ragged and red-nosed men in ordinary dress. Above the latter group fluttered a grimy banner inscribed: "The Isle of Wight Symphony Orchestra."

I had found it!

It, also, had found me. The conductor, catching sight of my fiddle-case, rushed at me in delight, leaving his band to get on as best they might with "Over the Waves," known among musicians of my class as "Sober at Last" (from the Spanish!).

"You're on our side!" he shouted.

"No, I'm not!" said I.

The town band was blaring forth "The Gondoliers" in the teeth of "Sober at Last," and my sole desire was to rush away and hide my ears from that ungodly row. I was in the act of doing so, when something pulled me up sharply.

Standing nearby, a very pretty girl about my own age was surveying me with interest. It struck me immediately that I had never seen any human being quite so attractive as that girl.

"Come on, come on, come on!" the conductor pleaded. "They're beating us hollow."

With my eyes on the girl, I took out my fiddle, joined the seedy group about the banner and scraped away furiously at "Sober at Last."

By now the town band had finished their first piece, but they gave themselves no rest, plunging straight into "Does He Drink?" or more correctly, "Morning, Noon and Night." Our conductor in turn, his face wreathed in delighted smiles, flung us into "Blasted Great Lumps of Fat," better known to the poor ignorant public as the Soldiers' Chorus from *Faust*.

Louder and louder grew that idiot din. The clatter of milk-cans being unloaded off a train would have been like the sweetest lullaby beside it. The bursting faces of the town band were shining with sweat, and even the cavernous pallid ones of the Symphony Orchestra were showing alarming signs of blood-pressure. The town band had the advantage of owning more brasses, but hunger had given our side better wind.

Then when we were in the middle of "Life on a Steamer" (you might call it Handel's *Largo*), and still going strongly while our opponents were beginning to show that they were feeling the pace, the match came to an end. Two large policemen arrived on the scene and, by gesture rather than command

—for even their voices were completely inaudible—
turned the Symphony Orchestra off the green. Glow-
ering, and snarling fearful threats, we stalked off,
leaving the now almost deflated town band in possession.

Mr. Weldon Russell who, as well as being manager, was also our *bottler,* or conductor, was most
indignant. He had arrived that morning to occupy
the Symphony Orchestra's usual pitch, only to find
it already taken up by the enemy. He had protested,
but, finding that useless, had thereupon flung the
full weight of his buskers' lungs into the issue in a
gallant attempt to blow the town band bodily from
their unrightful place. To be now driven off like
an interloper was the last straw to his *amour propre.*

I don't think either the town band or the Symphony Orchestra would have worried very much
about any aspersions cast upon their gentility, but
Mr. Russell felt he owed it to himself to justify his
followers. He wrote a very restrained and dignified
letter to the local paper, which was printed the following day, accusing the town band of ungentle-
manly conduct, and darkly suggesting that there
were others in the town who were not only superior
musicians but who could teach them the niceties of
deportment as well.

As far as I was concerned, there was no sequel to
the Battle of the Cliffs. In loyalty to my side, I
walked off the field with them, but I hurried back
as quickly as I could and sought out the girl who

had been the unconscious cause of my entry into the battle. We looked at one another and smiled.

"Did you ever hear such a row in your life?" I asked.

"It was funny," she said, then looked at me appraisingly. "You're young for a busker."

"I don't quite know if I am one yet," I replied. "Do you live here?"

"Yes."

"Good," I said boldly. "I'll start busking here, then."

And so it was. I stayed on in Shanklin for three months. For the first time in my life I was in love —the kind of inexpressibly exalted, spiritual love of adolescence. I would have walked miles—and did —to listen to the first words in her quiet voice, to see her sudden smile. I literally worshiped her, and the great social gulf between us—her folk were decent, dull tradespeople—intensified my rapt idolatry. What I had seen and done in the few years behind me had not left me ignorant of the things of the flesh, but for her I was as innocent in thought and deed as a young nun. In the pale soft light of her presence, I attained to a kind of ecstasy of purity.

I cannot doubt that it was a very ordinary and hoydenish affair, but it had immense value in my development. I like to think that it began to make me something different from the impossible hobble-dehoy I had been before, that it set my mind groping towards some conception of beauty. Of one thing I am certain: I was not so uncouth a savage when I left Shanklin as when I went there.

Thirty years later I revisited the town, this time under less ludicrous circumstances as director of my Ladies' Hussar Band. In the years between, I had not forgotten the somersaulting of my adolescent emotions, and made discreet inquiries about the object of them. It appeared that she was married to a prosperous tradesman and kept a shop.

I sought out the shop, and went in and bought something. I knew her immediately, and my voice faltered as I spoke to her. In my eyes she was still unchanged. The same charm of voice and look were there as had worked such damage on me on the day of the Battle of the Cliffs thirty years before. In all essentials she was the same young girl who had smiled at me on that distant, mad afternoon. I fumbled with my purchase, staring at her foolishly.

"Your change," she said. "Thank you."

It was almost a reproof. I took my change and left the shop. If she had remained unchanged, apparently I hadn't. She had not recognized me.

*   *   *

Until I was about seventeen, I wore my hair closely cropped, as was the fashion among young gentlemen of my acquaintance for reasons connected more with hygiene than becomingness. But one day

I was playing somewhere and found my accompanist to be a person of original ideas.

This was an entertainer called Clifton Barrett, whose name, by the way, is still to be seen on the clock outside the *Blue Posts* public house in Tottenham Court Road. He explained to me in the kindest manner that, although I played well enough, my appearance, with my peculiar clothing and bristling skull, was not reassuring to my audience, and suggested that I lost a great deal of well-merited applause because those listening to me thought it wiser not to clap their hands but keep them clutched firmly about their purses and watch-chains.

It was a piece of advice which struck me as eminently reasonable, for I was not immune to the musician's rooted belief that I never did get all the applause I deserved, and I agreed to let my hair grow long as a preliminary to respectability.

The result, however, was very different from that which we had expected. Instead of rich flowing tresses such as one sees in the self-portrait of Albrecht Dürer, I sprouted a crop of thick black spines which stuck straight out from my head in a wiry mop. Things had gone from bad to worse as far as the search for respectability was concerned. I had looked like a jailbird before; now I looked like a dervish.

By this time, however, Clifton Barrett had constituted himself my manager. He examined me reflectively under drooping eyelids.

"I see you," he said in the faraway voice of a prophet, "on the stage at the Palladium—Signor Petulini, the Violin Wizard. The people are howling for a fifth encore."

He looked at me again and shook his head disappointedly.

"No, they're not," he said sadly. Then: "I've got it! The Untamed Wild-Man Violinist! They'll eat you. You're every bit as wild as the Man from Borneo, but you can play the fiddle! You'll be the sensation of the century!"

I am comforted to think that very few people ever heard of me in that rôle, and fewer saw the Untamed Violinist in the flesh, but among those who did I was, without the shadow of a doubt, a sensation of the first magnitude.

Clifton Barrett was a first-rate showman. When we got an engagement and our turn came to perform, he would first of all go on the platform alone and give a lurid description of my horrible habits and ferocious disposition. Then, when the audience had been worked up into a suitable state of uneasiness and expectancy, I was led on—yes, literally led on! For round my neck was a steel collar, attached to a long chain, the other end of which Barrett held tightly grasped.

I would snarl and scowl awhile at the audience, and they inevitably would gasp in unquiet amazement, their mouths and eyes forming ranks of little round O's. When it was time to start our performance, Barrett would chain me to one of the piano legs, and we would play with the maximum of abandon. I am sure it was most impressive.

When we got engagements at affairs given under the patronage of local bigwigs, we were generally invited to the house of the patron, where I was naturally the center of interest.

Barrett used to explain that I had been reared in a very hot climate, so I was usually given hasty permission to squat or lie on the hearthrug before a grilling fire, and sometimes Barrett would, with serious intentness for my comfort, bring in a truss of straw to make me more at home. There I would crouch, and, as the evening wore on and I grew hotter and hotter, I found less and less difficulty in making my scowl convincingly savage.

Of course Barrett had given it out that I was quite unacquainted with the uses of plates, knives and forks, so the ladies of the party would feed me by hand; this, as they thought, at grave risk to themselves. . . . My bite was supposed to be poisonous!

It was amusing enough, but the sort of situation off which the humor wore very quickly. I could have murdered Barrett on one occasion when he tried to start a new legend about me to the effect that I would eat nothing but raw meat! I was not sorry when we decided to let the Untamed Violinist expire quietly. Ever since I have nourished a feeling of brotherly pity for the poor wretches of freaks who

appear in side-shows at circuses. It is pleasant to
know yourself different from the herd—but not too
different.

*   *   *

What extraordinarily civilizing implements are
these common articles, the brush and comb! After
the close of the Wild Man episode, I left my hair
long and bought the first brush and comb I had ever
owned. With these in my fumbling, inexpert hands
I coerced my bristling mop into a somewhat less
barbaric style of hairdressing. With my earrings
and careless form of dressing, I believe I might have
fitted the part of Signor Petulini that Clifton Barrett had first invented for me.

There followed a period during which I followed
faithfully the ancient tradition of the Prastermengro. I wandered the length and breadth of England
playing at fairs and village weddings. It was a
hard wild life, but a good life. I was grown-up
now, older than my years. In my own eyes, my
appearance was uncouth enough, but women seemed
to think me a picturesque figure in my checked
trousers, velvet jacket and flowing silk neckerchief,
and they had an embarrassing habit of paying me
ostentatious attentions to rouse the jealousy of their
rustic cavaliers and bring them up to the scratch. I
had my share of assaults and sudden escapes and
fights.

It toughened me. I was fitter and fleeter than
most of the yokels, and I generally came off best.

Not always, though. On one occasion I had drifted back to that tough district of Northeast London, and was fiddling away cheerfully at that accursed game of kiss-in-the-ring, when a girl selected me as her partner. I duly caught and kissed her and was about to resume playing again, when a hard-boiled battered-looking man grabbed me by the arm.

"Here, you!" he growled. "Nobody kisses my gel but me, see?"

I knew what was blowing up, and I was alert for it.

"You're welcome," I retorted somewhat unwisely.

"And you're welcome to *this!*" he said, still more unwisely, for it gave me warning of the vicious swing he let out at my head. I ducked my head and slipped the blow.

Even as I did so, it occurred to me that the man's face was familiar. I couldn't quite place it—but that wasn't worrying me at the moment. As I slipped his punch, I let him have my right on the side of his jaw. He went back a pace or two, then an indescribable grin spread over his face. With his fists weaving intricate patterns in the air, he came at me.

"Go on, Billy!" said a voice. "Kill the ——!"

Then I recognized my opponent. I had seen his face many times on the sports pages of newspapers. It was Billy Plimmer. He was then, if I remember right, lightweight champion of England.

It was clearly a moment that called for sudden escape rather than quick assault. Nearby was a derelict tramcar which some of the fair-ground folk were using as a house. I jumped back, grabbed my fiddle, then was round the back of the old tramcar with the speed of a rabbit disappearing into its hole. I blessed my father for bringing us up to wear light shoes. Billy Plimmer did not catch me.

It was only one—and not the most eventful—of the alarums and excursions which entangled my life at that time. I remember it particularly, I think, because its protagonist was quite a figure of the period. It was certainly a rough epoch, but in many ways it was typical of the rest of my life. One afternoon I would be playing Gounod at some ultra-respectable concert. The same night I would be fiddling in the street or fair-ground.

One day I was playing in the street near Ealing, when a lady came up to me and interrupted the piece I was playing.

"You play very well," she said.

"Thank you."

"But your instrument is incredibly bad."

I looked at my poor old fiddle.

"Oh, I don't know. It stands up pretty well."

"You deserve a better instrument, and you shall have one. If you go to Hill's in Bond Street tomorrow you'll find a violin ready for you that will be more worthy of your talent."

I was thick-headed and suspicious.

"What's the catch?" I demanded. "How much is this new fiddle going to cost me?"

"Nothing, naturally. You have only to go and collect it. I am Mrs. Hill. Good day."

With that she walked away. I stared after her, frowning in puzzlement.

Next day I went to Bond Street and sought out Hill's. Sure enough, a selection of instruments was waiting my inspection. I chose a lovely instrument, which I still have today. It is valuable monetarily, but it has another value for me which is greater. I never met Mrs. Hill again. I never had an opportunity of telling her how much her kindly gift meant to me, or how it awoke the sense of gratitude in the ungrateful young boor who took the gift with so little grace.

*   *   *

Sunset one pleasant Saturday night found me playing outside the old *Bull and Bush* in Hampstead. An elderly lady was passing, when she stopped abruptly, listened for a moment or two, then passed on. A few minutes later, however, I noticed her standing a few yards away watching me. Presently she came forward.

"I like your playing," she observed. "I wonder if you'd like an engagement?"

"I don't know," I answered. "What is the engagement?"

She said that she was giving a ladies' luncheon

party in a certain restaurant and would like me to play on the veranda during the meal.

"All right, I'll be there," I said. "Who'll I ask for?"

"Lady Edward Churchill," she answered, smiled, shook my hand, and was gone.

I duly presented my incongruous person at the restaurant in question. A flunky, plainly in a state of extreme pain over the duty, took me upstairs to the room in which the luncheon was to be held. As he was about to show me in, I heard Lady Edward Churchill's voice from the other side of the half-opened door.

". . . But I tell you, my dear, he's the typical gypsy, and he plays beautifully. He's the most completely independent person I've ever met. He said he'd come and play, although I gave him no money and mentioned nothing about his fee—"

Someone else was in the act of making some disparaging retort, when I was shown in. The hostess greeted me charmingly. The luncheon passed off successfully, my music seemed to be enjoyed, and I left with a substantial fee.

Shortly afterwards I was again playing outside the *Bull and Bush* when Lady Edward Churchill appeared once more, this time accompanied by a young man. She talked to me pleasantly for a while, introducing me to her companion and, when she was leaving, slipped a sovereign into my hand.

This, however, savored overmuch of charity for

my liking. I sensed the peril to my status as a free-born Prastermengro. I gave my benefactor back the sovereign. Perhaps I was surly enough about it, but it was no more than the surliness of the inarticulate thing I was. I had demonstrated that I loved money less than my peculiar out-at-elbows honor.

Lady Edward Churchill appeared to be delighted. She turned excitedly to her companion and cried:

"There you are! Isn't it all just as I told you!"

Smiling, the young man agreed.

There was no doubt that the eminent lady had taken a decisive interest in me. From that time on, she had me performing at most of her brilliant parties, and she was kind enough to recommend me to her friends, through whom I got a succession of other society engagements. There is no doubt that, for my brief hour, I was the fashionable fetish of the moment. Quite apart from my playing, I was an object of interest. To these people I was a curiosity. They looked on me as they might on a fish with rouged lips and permanently-waved hair. Yes, undoubtedly I was a queer fish in Mayfair. Or, if you prefer the other metaphor, I was a fish out of water. As such, it was inevitable that I should be slung back into my proper element again. The slinging back came about in somewhat laughable fashion.

Staying with Lady Edward Churchill at the time

was a young Swiss woman of title. From the time of my "entry into Society," this young woman had been particularly energetic in applauding and praising my fiddling. At length she begged me to give her violin lessons, and I agreed.

Heaven knows I wasn't equipped to teach anybody anything at the time, but I worked hard enough at the job to have encompassed a better result in my pupil than appeared after our lessons had been going on every day for some weeks. The result, in fact, was exactly nil. When I was "teaching" she would stare, languishing, at me, without listening to a word I was saying. If I touched her fingers to try to school them in holding fiddle or bow, she would sigh and droop.

I was not a young man of such admirable modesty as to be blind to what was happening. Drooping and languishing were fashionable accomplishments of smart young ladies of the period, and paunchy Italian tenors were pestered by shoals of love-sick maidens. I was flattered, but still too much of an oaf to respond romantically. My development had not reached the stage when I could be amused. The situation merely made me uncomfortable.

The *dénouement* was really too ridiculous. One afternoon I was talking to Lady Edward Churchill, when the Countess came into the room. She looked from one of us to the other, then burst out in her execrable English:

"So! Dees ees vot ees going on! You vas making loave to my *fiancé!*"

We both stared at her aghast. Then I began to make strange noises of suppressed laughter. The notion of being betrothed to a daughter of the European nobility was altogether too great a strain on my good behavior, and the idea of dear old Lady Edward entertaining romantic thoughts about such as myself was—well! I began to roar with laughter.

Lady Edward, on the other hand, went first red, then white. I think that extraordinary accusation must have been the greatest shock of her life.

I am fairly certain that it was a situation for which the rules of deportment have no provision. Lady Edward, at all events, did not appear to know of the proper move, if there was one. She got weakly to her feet, then, with gathering indignation, gave the young lady one freezing look and sailed with all dignity through the open door.

To my shame, I was still struggling with my plebeian laughter. The Countess was gazing at me piteously, and it was clearly no time for delaying. I hurried out after Lady Edward, and slipped quietly into the street with my fiddle. I never went back, nor saw my benevolent patroness again.

I wonder what happened afterwards?

* * *

In my hand was a copy of *Era,* and I was taking a great deal of interest in an advertisement headed

"The Carl Gunthie Grand Opera Company," which announced a vacancy for a violinist in that body. The company was working in Australia, and there was a restless itch in my wandering feet. It seemed to me that one could slake quite a lot of one's wanderlust between Tilbury and Australia.

I applied, and got the job. The fare for steerage was, I discovered, £11. I had just over £12. That was good. I could go.

IV

AUSTRALIAN EXCURSION

In the last decade of Victoria's reign, I set sail. The boat was, I think, the *Orisava*. Aboard her, I met a man and a woman who were, like myself, making the trip under the ægis of Carl Gunthie— the baritone and soprano of the Grand Opera Company.

To modern eyes, that voyage in the steerage must seem almost barbarous, but to us passengers it did not seem that we were undergoing much hardship —to me least of all.

Our stamping-ground was restricted to a small space in the bows, where we were not only herded like sheep, but suffered the herding with the dumbness of sheep—fit emigrants to a wool-raising continent! Here we had our pathetic and sometimes disgusting recreations; here we ate; here, when the weather grew warmer, we slept: strange uncouth objects of incurious interest to the godlike cabin passengers on the celestial eminence of the boat-deck.

When meal times came round, the crew brought long tables and wooden forms out on our stretch of deck space, and we sat down to eat out of tin mugs and tin plates dumped on the uncovered deal of the tables. The food was vile—salt-beef stew which looked and tasted like strips of boiled goloshes, and biscuits riddled with weevils.

With the food as it was, it was no wonder that every one of us went through agonies of seasickness. Whether the weather was rough or smooth, our ill-used stomachs simply would not hold down that awful stew and biscuit. Meal times were orgies of vomiting. There would be a steady procession of English passengers to the side. But there were a lot of foreigners aboard as well—mostly Scandinavians and Germans—and they were not so particular. They would turn where they sat and bring it up on the deck. Sometimes they did not even turn.

Our sleeping quarters below were dark, airless and smelly. When we came into the Tropics, they became insufferable, and we crowded on deck to sleep.

This apparently was the usual custom, and the authorities were prepared for it. The deck space was divided by a rope, and each sex had to sleep in the half allotted to it. Deck hands patrolled the dividing-line by the rope to enforce the proprieties —a necessary precaution, for our blood was hot in these latitudes, and an indescribable atmosphere of repressed lust was about the unwashed bodies strewn in close-packed rows on the deck.

The deck hands strove with one another for jobs as watchmen. In that capacity, they had opportunities such as sailors dream of. Among the restless

femininity aboard were a certain number of hard-
boiled "pretty ladies" traveling out with the intention of plying their ancient trade in the mining
camps of the new continent. I am afraid that their
sisterhood was increased by the addition of several
women going out with better intentions before the
voyage was over.

At last we docked in Fremantle, where the baritone, the soprano and myself were met by Mr.
Gunthie in person. In appearance he bore a striking resemblance to that Australian of later days,
George Cook, the heavyweight boxer. He had the
most hugely developed neck and shoulders I have
ever seen on any man.

In those days there were no passports and little
immigration formality. Gunthie swept us majesti-
cally away with him. We kept asking him ques-
tions about his Grand Opera Company, and at last,
after a series of evasions, he told us about it.

He was a professional strong man and juggler,
but one day a great thing had happened to him. He
had heard the Soldiers' Chorus and, on being told
it was Grand Opera, had resolved to start an opera
company of his own as soon as he had enough
money. Recently he had had a windfall, and was
now carrying his ideal into practise. He had collected a company of outstanding operatic talent,
which with our advent was now complete.

"Who have you got to conduct?" I asked.

"Oh, I'll do that myself," he answered somewhat

surprisingly. "Anybody can stand there and waggle a stick. It's only to show you're the boss of the show, anyway!"

At this the soprano, who had been looking more and more dubious since we landed, looked as if she were on the point of bursting into tears.

In a tin-roofed shanty standing forlornly in a sandy plain outside Fremantle, we met the other members of the company. There was a harpist and a pianist (whose instrument was of the portable variety) and a contralto. The contralto was Gunthie's wife, and her adoption of the calling of vocalist was a recent event. Hitherto she had been a "bender" or acrobat. She could bend better than she could sing.

"Now we're all here!" announced Gunthie cheerfully.

I looked round at my fellow artists. So we were all here. This was the complete company. It was as well to know the worst.

"Now we're all here, we'd better start rehearsing our opera right away."

"What opera are we doing?" inquired the baritone.

"The one with the Soldiers' Chorus in it—*Faust*," said Gunthie. "Anybody know it?"

It turned out that I knew the best-known parts of the work, and that our unhappy soprano knew the Jewel Song. The others did not appear to have heard of *Faust*. The pianist, who could not play except by ear, volunteered to vamp accompaniments.

"That's grand," said Gunthie, obviously delighted at finding such operatic knowledge among his company. "While we're rehearsing, we'll give high-class concerts."

In that self-same tin shanty, we gave our first concert. Mrs. Gunthie had not yet developed any "high-class" additions to her repertoire, so she boomed out comic songs in a voice that was a rasping combination of Florrie Forde's and Chaliapin's, if one can imagine both these celebrities suffering from laryngitis. The baritone sang ballads. The soprano, who had really quite a good voice, sang her Jewel Song. I played my selections from *Faust,* with the pianist putting in a weird music-hall accompaniment. The harpist played halting arpeggios. It was awful.

The audience were the tougher element among the local miners. Most of them apparently had come along because they were too drunk to be quite sure where they were going. They gave us the "bird" with brutal unanimity—especially to the harpist. Used as I was to the hard schooling of the fair-ground, I was not much affected, but our unfortunate soprano was in tears.

Things began to warm up. Somebody threw a bottle at the baritone, and the outlook was serious. The audience were in a mood for wrecking the place, including the performers.

It was then that Gunthie showed his true greatness. He stepped in front of the shrinking baritone,
and in good round Australian told the audience just
what peculiarly abandoned Philistines they were.
His great chest stuck out. His neck bulged. He
challenged each man singly with a menacing eye.

It was extraordinarily interesting to watch. There
were hard cases in the audience, but Gunthie was
a still harder case. His assurance and his terrific
physical vigor dominated them as completely as if
they had been the company at a mothers' meeting.
He literally defied any one of them to say a word.
None of them did. When he turned his back on
them there was dead quiet.

Even Gunthie, however, knew better than to dish
up the same "high-class" fare as before. It was
significant that the next turn was made up of a series
of feats of strength by himself, culminating in juggling his weighty wife in a rickshaw. It was very
impressive. None of the audience dared do anything but applaud ecstatically.

When it was all over, Gunthie beamed on us.

"They liked it," he declared. "What did I tell
you? There's a public in Australia for high-class
stuff!"

We went to Perth, then little more than a village,
and gave our strange performance there, beginning
this time with Gunthie's invaluable strong-man act.
From there we made a round by camel and rickshaw of the mining camps about. It was a rich and

strange experience. Our audiences were consistently "tough," always violent and nearly always drunk, but it was wonderful to see how a man of Gunthie's type, with illimitable confidence based chiefly on physical strength, could alone dominate a crowd of the wildest men you could find anywhere. He even got a fair hearing for the harpist.

As we moved westward of Perth, we heard strange rumors. Ned Kelly, most famous of bushrangers, had been brought to justice as far back as 1880, after terrorizing New South Wales for years, but one or two of his gang—black fellows led by an aborigine named Black Jackie—had escaped to Queensland. It was now being whispered that Jackie himself was in this barren district west of Perth: that he had accomplished the almost incredible feat of trekking completely across the continent, though hounded at every step by the police and their aborigine trackers. It was said that the two companions who had done the journey with him had both been shot down, but that Jackie, alone and desperate, well-armed, was at large in the near vicinity.

As we approached a camp about 100 miles from Perth, the rumors intensified, and they were quickened with fear, for Black Jackie was known to have a number of lives to his account, including several of men who had hunted him.

We reached the camp which was our destination, and settled down in a ramshackle café-cum-store which had been converted for the time into a concert hall.

We gave our usual show. Next day I was wandering in a thicket nearby, when a miner who had been one of the audience the previous night passed me in a state of considerable excitement.

"They've got him! Black Jackie!" he shouted as he hurried past. "Up in the wood here. They've just gone after him!"

I went the way he had pointed. It was all very quiet. Then the sound of a shot impinged on the dead silence. I hurried on. In a pretty little glade I came on a little crowd of men. They were looking down at something that lay sprawled behind a log. It was the body of a black fellow. He was shot through the brain, and his pleasant enough, unremarkable face was streaked with fresh blood.

They had come up with him as he lay sleeping behind the fallen tree-trunk, and had given him no chance of adding to his list of murders. He was, I understand, actually the last bushranger in Australia to pay the penalty for his crimes.

*   *   *

Insensibly, the character of our performances began to deteriorate. More and more we began to play down to the level demanded by our audiences. Gunthie had been losing money on his more ambitious programs, and the adjustment to meet the taste of our listeners was necessary, though Gunthie was very bitter at having to modify his high-brow ideals.

Then an unexpected thing happened. In one camp we encountered a miner who had had a lucky strike. He had sold his claim and was worth a small fortune. Now, in the most convenient fashion, he fell madly in love with our woebegone soprano. He was something of a rough diamond, and she was rather frightened of him at first; so he took to making friends with the other members of the "Opera Company" to get them to put in good words for him with her. He stood treat lavishly, and gave expensive presents. The soprano became flattered and gave her admirer more encouragement. The climax was that, with a large gesture, he handed over a handsome sum of money to Gunthie to develop the Company along its original pretentious lines.

Clothed in a new dignity, we set out for Adelaide. It was symptomatic of our new status that we hired camels for only short stretches of the journey, going the major part by train. Our backer came with us.

Arriving in Adelaide, we played in town halls and such-like in the environs, bored audiences witnessing a spate of renderings of the Jewel Song. Gunthie, meantime, was in his element. Every day or so he acquired additions to the personnel. With the skeleton of a chorus and something that called itself an orchestra, we moved to Melbourne and played in the smaller towns and larger camps about what was then a very small city. Gunthie's dream came true. We did *Faust, The Bohemian Girl, The*

Rose of Castille and *Maritana*. The soprano was always the star, but no one objected to that. We all knew that she was now quite the most important person in our company.

Gunthie "conducted." That is to say he "waggled his stick to show he was the boss." But the orchestra was little affected. It was bad enough to be bad under any conductor, and none of us paid any attention to his beat in any case.

Our backer was cheerfully losing money like water. We took relatively good halls. Sometimes there were more people in the cast than in the auditorium, but we were all quite happy. The soprano blossomed forth with a fur coat and an incredibly sudden assurance of manner. We went back to the suburbs of Adelaide.

There decisively and finally the Carl Gunthie Grand Opera Company collapsed and wheezed out its last dying breath. The soprano ran away with the backer.

One by one, the newer members of the brotherhood dropped out, until we were left with practically the original nucleus. Gunthie looked both disappointed and relieved. I think he was already bored with Grand Opera, having discovered that not all of it was quite like the Soldiers' Chorus. After all, juggling was something he knew and understood, and he took a very proper pride in his particular art.

"It's concert work for us again," he announced

to us. "We'll hit it back to Melbourne. It's my home town, and we shan't starve there."

Back to Melbourne it was. At the beginning of the venture I had been receiving a princely £3 a week. From now on, I rarely got more than 10s.; and yet in those spacious days I suffered no hardship. Gunthie was passionately devoted to cards— not solely because of a sporting sense—and I could afford to lose up to half of my weekly wage without feeling the pinch. Be it noted that I invariably did lose it.

This wonder of economics was made possible by the prices of food in Australia at that time. One could buy an excellent meal with large quantities of mutton for threepence, and a milk-shake of powerful nutriment for a penny. I lived well and cheerfully. Ticky-beer was cheap and good.

Gunthie, now happily and unashamedly a juggler again, always won at cards. The more I saw him play, the more I became convinced that he had other talents besides juggling to keep him from starving when times were hard. Perhaps I was lucky in having little to gamble with.

"We're going to Sydney," he said abruptly one day.

"What for?" asked his wife.

"I'll tell you when I know myself," he replied cryptically.

Wisely, she did not press for any more details. We went to Sydney. Gradually a possible reason for the journey began to appear. In the gay, vulgar, exciting Sydney of those days there flourished a celebrity known as the Bristol Infant. He was an Englishman of tender years and truly infantile mind who had come into a fortune of some £30,000. Even among the most inveterate gamblers of Australia, he was recognized as the king-pin of plungers. He would bet on anything and play cards with anyone.

In the intervals of shipping aboard cargoes of more potent liquids, he had an eccentric whim for drinking Bovril-and-soda. To get into his good graces it was only necessary to order a Bovril-and-soda in his hearing from an astonished bartender. Gunthie became irresistibly attracted to this strange character, and they became bosom friends. I need not say that Gunthie assimilated notable quantities of Bovril-and-soda.

That versatile juggler had a somewhat seedy friend, an ex-solicitor, and nightly card-parties with these two, the Bristol Infant and myself became the rule. The stakes quickly became so high that, while the others were gambling in pounds, I was gambling in pennies. Judging by the number of pennies I lost, I imagine the Infant must have got rid of a considerable number of pounds.

What an incredible Infant it was! Like many other fourth-rate people, he had unlimited self-conceit. There was a famous black tracker of the day, with whom the Infant would have long-distance running matches. The black fellow would walk the

race to let the flabby and perspiring Infant win,
which pleased him mightily.

He also thought a good deal of himself as a boxer,
and would often put on the gloves with me. Invariably I gave him a good hiding, being constitu-
tionally averse to pandering to the conceit of fools,
and ended up by putting him out for a long count.
He would totter weakly to his feet. "Ah, you're too
good for me. I'm not fighting any more," I would
say. He would be delighted, and preen his feathers
before his covey of sycophants again.

Inevitably, he put money into Gunthie's projects.
The juggler, by this time, was all for making Australia opera-minded once more. The Grand Opera
Company was resuscitated, and its shaky old bones
were hung about with unexpected splendor. We
actually enjoyed our brief spell of glory before the
company expired again, and for a time we had with
us one of Australia's most famous singers: the baritone, Snazasel, who had acquired wide fame with
his singing of "Nazareth."

The second dying was not far off, however. The
Bristol Infant was convinced that he was a brilliant
singer, just as he was a splendid runner and boxer.
He made Gunthie put on *The Bohemian Girl* so
that he could play "Devil's Hoof."

That night there was nearly a riot as soon as
"Devil's Hoof" got properly going. The audience
were shouting "Rotten!" as one man every time the
Infant uttered a note. The manager of the hall was

in terror of his place being broken to bits. He objected in the strongest language to Gunthie, who went behind the scenes to warn "Devil's Hoof" not to show his face in front again.

"Can't you hear them? They're shouting 'Rotten!'"

"No, they're not. They're shouting 'Killarney.' They want me to sing it," said the Infant.

He did. There was a riot. And there and then the unquiet corpse of the Opera Company was buried for good.

Gunthie did not immediately go back to concert work. He had more profitable employment in hand. I took more and more engagements on my own, and had the pleasure of playing solos in the St. George's Hall in George Street. One night I went and saw the grand boxing match between Peter Jackson and Frank Slavin.

I still played cards with Gunthie. It meant losing my few shillings, but I was intrigued by the way in which he always came off best. One simply could not detect how he arranged it, and I was determined to find out.

Eventually I did. One night Gunthie became unwontedly communicative, and showed me his method of stacking the pack. It was very ingenious and I was flattered at this sign of his complete trust in me. Then it transpired later that he wanted me with him to travel on the boats plying to India and back. We should, he promised, live like kings on the proceeds of our card-playing. My qualification, he said, was that I "looked a mug."

But I wanted no more of Gunthie. Everywhere I had played cards in Australia—with Gunthie's crowd or the old-timers in the mining camps—I had lost steadily. Knowing myself to be a "mug" in actual fact as well as appearance, I had wanted to discover just how I had been fleeced. Now I knew. I would be a mug no longer.

"I'm getting a bit tired of Australia," I said to Gunthie. "I'm thinking of going back to England again."

"Please yourself, son," said the great man, and sighed regretfully. "I suppose I couldn't persuade you to change your mind about not working them India boats?"

"You're right," I said. "You couldn't."

Having made my decision, I set about finding some means of making that journey across the world. My total wealth amounted to no more than a few shillings. That, and my good fiddle, made by the philanthropic firm of Hill, of Bond Street.

I hung about the docks of Sydney, hoping for a job as a musician on one of the liners, but, in spite of Gunthie's assertion about my appearance, I looked such a complete cutthroat that decent leaders of ships' orchestras shrank from me.

Eventually I did get a job on a boat; but it was loading frozen mutton into the hold of a big German ship carrying passengers and cargo. The mutton was as hard as rock, and after a few days my soft hands were lumps of raw flesh. For over a week I worked as a stevedore, and many times as I shivered in that icy hold I looked at my bleeding hands and wondered if I should ever be able to play my fiddle again. But I knew that London was one of the vessel's ports of call. I had hopes.

I was lucky. At least, I suppose I was lucky. At any rate, I was engaged for the voyage by the Master-at-Arms as extra deck hand at a shilling a month. If I had had any inkling of what I should experience on that voyage, it is quite likely that I should have stayed on in Australia until I could pay my passage home.

The last I saw of the Bristol Infant was in the back room of a hotel. He was playing some childish variety of snooker for big stakes with a twister of more education, and probably less pity, than the inimitable Gunthie. Shortly afterwards, my boat, on the night tide, was bisecting the glittering circle of the harbor lights. I did not see either that prince of punters or that most bizarre of impresarios again.

V

LOG OF A HELL SHIP

I THINK my official position aboard was that of "general servant." My duties included holystoning the deck, painting the hull in calm weather slung over the side in a bo'sun's cradle, and keeping a watch.

The usual duration of a watch is, of course, four hours, with the two dog-watches of two hours each to allow rotation of the members of the crew on the various watches. My watch aboard that vessel began at eleven o'clock at night and did not finish until five in the morning.

My sleeping quarters were supposed to be in a cramped apartment, full of awkward corners, called, if I remember, "the lower forecastle"; but the place was so airless, so dark and damp, so vermin-ridden and thick with the stench of filthy humanity, that I seldom slept there throughout the voyage. I shared it with ten other down-and-outs, the veriest scum of humanity, who had been shipped aboard because eleven good seamen had jumped the ship at Sydney. The lordly A.B.'s slept in some other infinitely luxurious fo'c'stle.

In the bunk below mine was a Finn suffering

from a loathsome infectious disease. After we had been at sea for a couple of weeks, he went down under it and could not leave his bunk, where he lay sweating and continually moaning, occasionally breaking out into wild raving in his native tongue.

Almost from the start of the voyage, I did not attempt to face the vile squalor of that fo'c'stle. In the daylight hours, when I should have been sleeping, I wandered about, seeking for a corner where I might be alone and rest. To find such a spot in the restricted area where the crew might put their feet was impossible. And I was "general servant." They called me "Spider."

I would be straying about the deck, half-dead from sleeplessness after my watch, when someone in authority would catch sight of me. Then it would be:

"Here, Spider! Havin' a holiday? Let's see you holystone this bit of deck."

I was the lowest thing aboard. I got all the dirtiest, most stomach-turning jobs to do. Because I was under no one man in particular, I was anybody's slave.

For the use of our fo'c'stle, there was one lavatory. It was doorless, and my peculiar training had inhibited me against performing my bodily functions in public. I made and carried out elaborate plans for using the other lavatories on board, without being caught. Only because it was one of my more unpleasant duties to clean them out was this made possible. As for the sty designed for the use of the fo'c'stle, I was never asked to clean it; so it is certain that it was not cleaned throughout the voyage, for who was there lower than myself to perform this degrading task?

I was ignorant, wild, and rather queer. To me it seemed degrading to line up with one's plate for the disgusting food we got. It savored to me of begging. I preferred to steal food from the pantry.

The first hour of my watch, from eleven to midnight, I would play cards. The officer of the watch did not appear. I had orders to waken him at the times of inspection. Being a high personage aboard, he was entitled to the incredible privilege of sleep.

At twelve, I was joined by one who seemed to me the only human being aboard. He was an A.B., a Scotsman, and the sole friend I had. After reporting on the bridge, I could indulge in the supreme luxury of sleeping for an hour, while Jock watched. I did so on the settee of the saloon.

At one Jock woke me, and I kept awake while he slept. For the next hour I had to keep awake, and I did so by catching rats in the pantry where I went to make cocoa for the officer on the bridge. In the intervals of catching the rats, I made my best meal of the day.

At two, I woke Jock, for it was a dangerous time from now on to attempt to sleep. We would play cards for matches, and talk, and sometimes I would play Scots airs for him on the fiddle—very softly.

I am sure Jock never realized what his companionship meant to me during that nightmare voyage. Perhaps it saved my sanity. I wonder if he was a very low type of man to have had any truck with such as I?

Naturally this system of having but one hour's sleep out of the twenty-four could not go on for long. There came a time when I was forced to capitulate and brave the filth and the odor of the lower fo'c'stle. My desire for privacy was understandable as regards the lavatory, but it went farther than that. Something in my nature made me revolt against undressing—that is to say, partly undressing —along with the other derelicts in the fo'c'stle. So I hung rags and strips of old blanket in front of my bunk and crawled in behind the barrier like an animal into its hole. The foul air could not keep me awake. The snoring of the men about me could not. Not even the painful breathing and low mumbling of the sick man in the bunk below me could retard my exhausted mind and body from slipping deep into sleep.

I awakened in a dead silence. Peering about me through my curtain of rags, I could see that all the other bunks were empty. It was matter for relief, yet I felt uneasy. The silence which should have soothed me, disquieted me.

Abruptly I realized the cause. The Finn in the bunk below me had ceased his raving. I climbed out of my bunk, and, as I dropped to the floor,

I saw the Finn. He was dead, with his eyes staring and jaw dropped.

They buried him the same day. The other men would not go back into the fo'c'stle for fear of infection, although why they should fear it more after the Finn's death than before, I could not fathom.

My sleep had not nearly made up for all the rest I had missed since coming aboard. Like the others, I was afraid of infection, but the longing for sleep was stronger than my fear; and there was the fo'c'stle empty of the filthy bodies of my fellows. I went below and slunk behind my screen of rags. I slept.

Choking and coughing, I awoke. The apartment was full of acrid yellow smoke. My lungs were full of the fumes of burning sulfur. I leaped out of my bunk and blundered towards the door. It was locked. Coughing till I vomited, I wrestled with the unmoving door, and banged on it with my fists and tried to shout.

In the middle of the floor, I saw the glow of the burning sulfur. It was on a shovel. The smolder of it through the heavy yellow fog was inexpressibly weird.

I kicked the shovel over and stamped on the burning sulfur, but it was extraordinarily difficult to put it out. I flung myself at the door again. I coughed and coughed, and it seemed as though my lungs were being bitten out by those ghastly fumes and that I must vomit them up at any moment. I was very light-headed. The dark fo'c'stle, wreathed in great flying swaths of yellow smoke, swirled round my head, rotating faster and faster.

I beat at the door till my hands were broken and bloody. It seemed impossible that nobody could hear me: impossible but true. No easy death, this. No gentle sinking into nothingness on the wings of weakness. The weaker I felt, the nearer I came towards unconsciousness, the greater choking torture I suffered.

Then, away at the other end of the world, through an infinite corridor of half-consciousness, I heard a voice. It came from the other side of the door. I beat at the door again with the crazy energy of a final frenzy. There was a small click. A sniff of fetid life-giving air came to me as the door opened inwards, knocking me down. I coughed, and then I fainted.

I took very little hurt from my experience, although I heard from the ship's doctor that I had had a very narrow escape from being suffocated. Very wisely, it had been decided to fumigate the fo'c'stle after the Finn's death, and I, sleeping behind my screen of rags, had remained unnoticed when they were busy lighting the sulfur and hermetically sealing up the apartment. I very nearly paid with my life for my stolen sleep.

From then on, I kept out of the fo'c'stle altogether. At odd times I slept unashamedly and unrepentantly on the tops of hatches abovedecks. It meant being kicked into wakefulness dozens of times and sent to do some job or other, and it was little sleep I stole for the rest of the voyage, but I had good reason to prefer that to the sepulcher below.

Presently I fell foul of the pantryman. I had been helping myself to food from the pantry since the beginning of the trip, and he must have noticed the thefts. There came a watch when, during the preparation of cocoa for the officer on the bridge, I was eating beans from a tin with a spoon. Without warning, the door of the pantry was flung open, and the fat German pantryman charged in on me.

He flung a mouthful of furious German at me, spat in my face and, lifting a heavy pot, made a murderous swipe at my head. I ducked and backed into a corner. My position was a serious one. He was much heavier than I, and in that confined space could have almost smothered me by sheer force of weight. I flung the tin of beans at him.

It struck him just above one eye and the mess of beans spewed itself down one cheek. It checked him just long enough for my purpose. I smashed my right to his jaw and my left to his stomach. As he half doubled up, I hit him on the jaw again. He went down, and the pot he held slid across the floor. I dodged round him and got my back to the door.

Blowing, he got to his feet and came for me again with his fists. But in that sort of scrapping, the fair-grounds had taught me more than the sea had taught him. I kept him at a distance with my left and punished him with my right until his fine rage had cooled down completely. He was the type just built for being hit about the body, and I did not spare it. After about ten minutes, I finished him off with a swing to the solar plexus that left him squirming on the floor, able to get up but not wanting any more.

My watch finished, I sought out a hatch and slept. My awakening was a rude one. I was hauled bodily off the hatch, and, as my body thumped on the deck, a heavy boot kicked me in the back.

It was the Master-at-Arms, one of that blond, beefy type of German which wrestles and does feats of strength at music halls—a giant of a man, and no friend of mine.

"So!" he growled. "You're de great fighting man, eh? Get up an' show what you can do."

I got up. As I was doing so, he swung his boot at my face. But I had seen that trick before. I dodged and jumped back on my toes. He flung himself at me, and he did not come at me with his fists. His hands were open, claw-like, a typical wrestler's attitude.

I did not mean to get between these arms if I could help it. I brought my right across and down like a hammer, striking his left inwards with the bone of my forearm. As he slewed round, I hit him over his shoulder on the side of his jaw.

He came at me again. Again I knocked his arm

inwards and landed on his face; this time flush on his left eye. So it went on, each of us performing the same maneuvers—but not for long. He was so much bigger and stronger than I that it was merely a matter of time before he got to close quarters and could ram home his advantage. By this time, his injured eye had swollen badly, and he was mad with pain and rage.

He grabbed me by one arm and pulled me to him. With his other hand he gripped me by both lapels of the ragged jacket I was wearing.

"Now!" he said, and jammed me against the bulwark with such force that it seemed to me as if every bone in my body had been shaken out of its proper place.

Then he proceeded literally to wipe the floor with me. He was familiar with a wide variety of ferocious wrestling holds, and he demonstrated the lot on my carcase. He flung me over his shoulder on to the deck, jumped on me, picked me up, and flung me into the scuppers, picked me up again and tied me into a knot, untied me agonizingly, and flung me down again. As a finale, he got me arched over the same hatch on which I had been sleeping and, holding me helpless with one hand, pounded my face with the other.

I was numb and only semi-conscious, past feeling pain, when I heard a sharp voice speaking, and at the same moment I was released. I could not move, but lay where I was on the hatch, with my back bent over it like a bow.

There was another order, and many hands lifted me up.

I do not know what happened to me immediately after that; but, when I awoke, I was lying—not in my filthy bunk in the fo'c'stle, but between starched white sheets in the passenger's sick-bay.

From that moment onwards, my troubles were over. Apparently what had happened was that one of the passengers had seen the fight, and immediately gone to the Captain and told him that a youth among the crew—I was only seventeen at the time —was being unmercifully beaten up by the Master-at-Arms. The second officer had been sent instantly to stop the massacre, and I, thanks to the indignant demands of the passenger who had witnessed the business, was installed in the clean white splendor of the sick-bay.

I was a nasty mess when they brought me in, and it was feared that I was seriously injured; but it turned out that apart from a couple of broken ribs my hurts looked and felt worse than they were.

When I was ready to be up and about again, I discovered myself to be an object of intense interest and sympathy among the passengers. The rags I had been wearing on coming aboard had been finally torn to small pieces by the hands of the Master-at-Arms. I took one look at them, and flung them overboard. Upon which the passengers held a drive among themselves which provided me with a strange collection of garments. I had the jacket of a man half my size, and the trousers of a man twice my size, and shoes and shirts equally assorted; but they were clean and whole, and I was glad of them.

I did not go forward again. An empty cabin was found for me in the passengers' quarters, and, during the remainder of the voyage, I paid with my fiddling for my bunk and board and the clothes I had been given.

What orgies of sleep I had! What banquets—not of beans, but of exactly similar food to that which the Captain himself was eating! During the days I loafed consistently. In the evenings I played solos. It was a good life.

My fractured ribs mended quickly. By the time we docked at Tilbury I was as good as new again. As for the Master-at-Arms, my benefactors among the passengers were for making him suffer a host of dreadful penalties for the damage he had done to my person; but whether he got into serious trouble over the affair or not, I never found out.

I am not sentimental. I have been out of England often enough to be glad to return to her. But I do not get a lump in my throat and a stinging moistness in my eyes when I see her white bulwarks defying the sea. When I caught my first glimpse of her cliffs near the end of that voyage, however, jutting up through the gloom and driving rain of

a typical Channel evening, I had a number of un-
wonted symptoms which might, if allowed, have
developed into the authentic sob and tear of the
returned wanderer. In other words, it was good to
be back.

VI

THE ROADS OF YOUTH

BACK in London once more, I was met at Fen-church Street Station by a great friend of mine, a youth of about my own age who had been inaptly christened with the aristocratic name of Basil.

He was a rather extraordinary person. His mother was a gypsy woman, and his father kept a large glass factory not a thousand miles from London Bridge. Basil Senior had fallen in love with his future wife and had taken her from the van to marry her. But the young bride had never lived in a house before and, after many changes of residence, the couple settled down in a few vacant rooms above the glass factory. Perched up there in isolation, she was able to give her ego full expression—or at least fuller expression than it would be allowed in a sub-urban bungalow.

I was often a guest at that curious establishment. There were coal and faggots piled on the floor of the kitchen. Rabbits scuttled about under the queer assortment of rubbish that served for furniture. Fowls roosted on chair-backs and bedposts.

The bridegroom was so much in love that he was ready to endure anything; but to the bride even these free and easy arrangements were not free and easy enough. I think she must have had an authentic passion for the "wind on the heath."

She bore with things as they were for years, but was never completely happy; and it was with a keen delight that she watched her son, Basil, growing up into a typical gypsy. He had all the uncommon outlook and talents of her people; none of those of her husband. The latter, making a despairing last effort to switch his son on to the paths of respectability and a normal healthy British code of living, put him into the glass factory; and that was Basil's irksome situation at the time of meeting me after my return from Australia. The outcome was unexpected.

I was bound for Wembley, where my parents were living. We went from Fenchurch Street to Baker Street Station, where we changed. It was at Baker Street that we discovered that my precious fiddle (which comprised my total luggage) was missing.

We hurried back to Fenchurch Street, and unhopefully sought out a seat where we had sat talking while waiting for our train to Baker Street. And there on the seat where we had left it was my fiddle case, with the fiddle inside. In view of the busy state of the station, we were both affected by a sense of the miraculous.

Basil duly set me on my way. For some time

afterwards I did not see him, but his subsequent history is interesting.

His father, wishing to instil a proper sense of responsibility into Basil, left him in charge of the factory shortly afterwards when he had to be absent for some days. Now part of Basil's duties during this spell of authority was to design the ornamentation for various glassware; a task at which he was very good; and it so happened that an order had come in for a large number of tumblers from a public house called the *Adam and Eve*. The ornamentation on these glasses, for which Basil had made the original design, was of two unclad but unexceptionable figures representing Adam and Eve standing under a conventional apple tree.

Left to his own devices, Basil, in the manner of all true artists, became dissatisfied with his first design. His precocious imagination promptly suggested a means of brightening it up. He set about elaborating the simple scene of Adam and Eve under the apple tree; and, when he had done so, it was a brighter scene indeed, if hardly so ingenuous as it had been before.

The enlivened design was faithfully cut into each of the large consignment of glasses for the *Adam and Eve,* and the glasses were delivered.

The customers at the public house were not slow in noticing the alterations made in the sober early design; and the new version was much to their liking. Custom improved noticeably for a while, and then there started an epidemic of thefts of tumblers from the bar. At this point, the management found out what had happened. The word was passed on to the glass factory, and Basil was unmasked.

His father, more in sorrow than in anger, cast him forth. Self-containedly, Basil bade his mother farewell, telling her he would naturally and with a good heart take to the caravans of her people, and left.

It was the final straw to his mother's discontent. Although she lived in an establishment of such eccentricity that any earnest Bohemian from Bloomsbury would have gone green with envy to see it, she missed the carefree wandering of her girlhood. She had as much freedom now as then; but she longed intensely for the old change and movement. Shortly afterwards, she, too, took to the caravans. Some years afterwards I saw her on a fair-ground in the Midlands. Basil was with her, and mother and son were plying a lucrative and quite irreproachable trade in horse-dealing. They were both supremely at peace with the world.

* * *

Not long after my return from Australia, I became a member of the Egyptian Band which played at the Earl's Court Exhibition. After some time of this, however, I left the, for me, curiously appropriate Egyptian Band, and went to Ilfracombe at the invitation of a friend of mine named Ronalds.

Ronalds at the time was entertainment manager for a large London store, and had been sent down to Ilfracombe in the same capacity at the request of a number of musical enthusiasts in the town, who were eager to provide good entertainment for the community. Ronalds, having been engaged for this object, had in turn recommended me as one who could play solos and lead the orchestra he had collected down there in the West.

I had known Ronalds in his earlier years when he had been a ventriloquist and conjurer at fairs. He was undoubtedly the world's worst ventriloquist, but his turn was always popular. He simply could not speak without glaringly moving his expressive lips, but he got round this admittedly large difficulty quite simply. When his dummy was supposed to be singing or doing anything equally complicated vocally, he simply held the dummy in front of him so that his own face was completely hidden and sang lustily. This shift was not always possible, of course, but Ronalds was equal to anything. When the dummy was supposed to be speaking and his own mouth was opening and shutting flagrantly, he would make the dummy point at him and pipe out accusingly:

"I saw you, Ronalds! I saw 'em move!"

That, I contend, smacks unmistakably of true genius. . . .

I arrived in Ilfracombe, a dour, suspicious illiterate of eighteen or so. Travel, far from broadening my mind, had crystallized in it a callow grace-lessness, a subconscious grudging admission of my own inferiority. I could not know that that placid Devon town was to be the unfitting scene for what was to be perhaps the most eventful period of my life.

My loutishness, which was compounded half of sensitiveness, half of pure ungraciousness, showed itself at the very first concert at which I played. A local pianist was playing my accompaniments, and he played as many wrong notes as right ones. As might be imagined, the fiddling suffered as much as the pianoforte, as a result; and I was convinced in my admittedly queer mind that the blame would be cast on the new fiddler. I was overcome with an extremity of shame. While the applause for my first solo was still ringing out, I ran off the stage, my eyes full of hot tears.

I bumped straight into that large and genial comedian, Walter Bently.

"Where are you off to?" he demanded.

"It's awful! It's awful!" was all I could answer.

"It's all right," he retorted. "Come on, now. Get back to that stage and take your encore."

I was still struggling to get past his bulk, when he winked at a man who was with him. Together, they lifted me and carried me bodily back in front of the audience. Sullenly I played through my encore, then escaped.

That night I wandered about the cliff-tops alone.

I was sure I was a laughing-stock among all these folk like Bently who seemed on the surface to be so kindly and encouraging. I was sure they were making sly jokes about me as soon as I was out of ear-shot. I was sure the audience were smiling and saying sarcastic things about my poor playing. I seriously contemplated suicide that night. That, no doubt, seems to suggest more than one bat in a very unstable belfry; but I myself like to think that the only time I ever debated suicide with myself was when I felt my playing had been poor. I like to think that the artist who is disproportionately cast down over his art is a less contemptible being than a man who wants to end his life because he has lost a little money and found life too much for him.

Fortunately a new pianist arrived next day from London—fortunately, for who knows what might have happened to me had the suicide-driving pianist remained? I settled down more amiably, and with good reason, for the people who were running the concerts were the pleasantest in the world, the prime movers being two well-known citizens, Commander Eadie and Dr. Gardiner, whose enthusiasm for music must have cost them a good deal of money, for these Ilfracombe concerts were much too good and expensive to pay for themselves.

Commander Eadie took a great deal of interest in me—or rather, in my playing. There were a number of hoydenish young women at the concerts who made clumsy advances to me. These the Commander shooed away, and generally kept me from bad or unelevating company. I believe he thought I might train into a really worth-while artist, and I think my personality and background, so different from the usual English model, intrigued him as a study.

Among other pleasant and cultured people he introduced me to were a mother and daughter of the name of Taylor. I did not realize it at the time, but the day I met these charming people was one of the most important in my life.

Mrs. Taylor was the widow of an Army officer, and, as a marked exception to the rule of such, was passionately devoted to all the arts. I owe her an incalculable debt of gratitude. She contrived my apotheosis. She civilized me.

When I met her first, I could neither read nor write. My vocabulary was so limited and my English so bad that I was taken by many people for a foreigner, an impression which my long hair and swarthiness did nothing to alter. I think she pitied me for my limitations, for my strangeness and the loneliness of my suspicious sullen spirit. She was kind to me. She would ask me to her house, and I would talk to her as I had never talked to anyone before, save perhaps my mother.

The great moment came one afternoon just after I had finished having tea with her and her daughter. On one wall was a strip of embroidered silk with some words worked on it in colored thread. The bright prettiness of it caught my eye. I knew that the cabalistic signs formed by these twists of colored thread formed those inconceivably learned abstractions known as Words. I knew that from dumb staring at print in the past.

It happened that, at that moment, the armor of my boorishness was down, slipped from me, unnoticed, by the graciousness of these two women. Child-like, the bright thing had caught my eye and fascinated it. I pointed at it and said idly:

"Those words written on the silk there: what do they mean?"

She gave me a quick enigmatic look, then began to repeat slowly:

"Come, fill the cup, and in the Fire of Spring
The Winter Garment of Repentance fling:
The Bird of Time has but a little way
To fly—and lo! the Bird is on the Wing."

I said reflectively:

"I like that. What's it from?"

"It's a verse from *The Rubáiyát* of Omar Khayyám. He was a Persian poet. A man called Fitzgerald made a wonderful translation of the poem into English."

"How many verses are there in the poem?" I asked.

"Oh, something over seventy."

I was silent for a moment; then I said slowly:
"I wish I could read. . . ."

Mrs. Taylor leaned forward.

"How would you like me to teach you?"

My heart beat fast. Earlier, I had always shunned the labor of plowing through the alphabet, but the knowledge at that moment that there were millions of people who had the key to such beauty as I saw suddenly revealed in the stanza made me realize in a flash how I had always been unconsciously aching for lack of that beauty, unrecognized and hitherto unsought, which I must now take unto myself or spiritually perish.

"If you'd do that, isn't there something I could do for you to make it even?" I stammered. "Miss Taylor plays the piano and is fond of music. Couldn't I give her violin lessons?"

Mrs. Taylor smiled.

"I think that would be a splendid arrangement," she said.

Such indeed it was. I was hardly competent to be a professional music teacher, but I passed on to my pupil the learning I had received from my father—and there are worse ways of learning to fiddle than the gypsy way. I learned and taught to keep the bow at right angles to the strings, without sickening myself of it by insisting on holding the bow or fiddle-neck in any accepted manner. No practising was allowed while the fingers were hot, and the fingers of the left hand were forbidden to press too tightly or to become tense. By this means the "cushions" of the finger-tips were kept free from calluses, and the tone was not permitted to become harsh.

I labored painfully through my alphabet and the spelling of "cat" and "dog." I wrestled with the rudiments of grammar. I began to write simple sentences in big round characters. I learned the joy of being able to look admiringly at my own name, written by my own hand. I could with complacence watch men practising the hitherto esoteric art of reading the newspapers, knowing myself able to understand at least a portion of what they were reading. I was like a child who has mastered the lore of telling the time from a clock face.

Early, I girded my wits to struggle with the deciphering of *The Rubáiyát*. It was not too difficult a task, for, the proper names apart, the language was simple in the main and the continual repetition of certain words such as "rose" and "cup," and the duplication of the same images, saved me from overmuch memorizing. It was a proud day for me when I could read a new stanza straight off and understand every word, and a black one when a catchy verse forced me to call in Mrs. Taylor's help for all but the monosyllables.

When at length I could get along fairly well with the aid of a dictionary, I was seized with a voracious lust for reading. I had acquired a power of superb potentialities, and I could not satiate myself with using it. My teacher saw the danger of my developing a puerile taste in reading-matter, and was careful to see that I read nothing but worthy books from the very start.

The circumstances of the moment had fortunately made me unwontedly amenable, and I did exactly as she prescribed. After the traditional usage, I read the writers of the eighteenth century, but they were a more full-blooded company, I imagine, than are usually prescribed for schoolboys. I read *Tristram Shandy,* and the picaresque novels of Smollett. I devoured most of Swift, all of Fielding, and Gibbon's *Decline and Fall;* as well as Trollope's *The Warden,* Emily Brontë's *Wuthering Heights* and Darwin's *Origin of Species.* All these within a very few weeks.

Reading as much as I did and speaking so little, it was inevitable that words which I could recognize in print I found very unwieldy in conversation. I pronounced the word "character" as written, for instance, and, more curiously, "criminal" as "sriminal." Mrs. Taylor, however, took infinite pains to keep my pronunciation approximately correct. I learned the golden rule of never using for effect a word that one is in any way doubtful about pronouncing.

Time passed blissfully. I spent nearly all my leisure hours in reading.

One day as I was leaving Mrs. Taylor's house after the usual violin lesson, she said to me:

"There's a violin teacher wanted in a girl's school here. Do you think you would like to become a school teacher?"

I gaped.

"What? Me a school teacher!"

"Why not? My daughter says you teach very well. Anyway, if you want to take it on, I shall recommend you."

I muttered some thanks and left. Within a few days the incredible thing came about. I was standing, tongue-tied and hot, before a class of giggling schoolgirls. It was quite a good school, and anything more out of place there than my wild-looking self could not be imagined.

There was no discipline when I taught. My youth and my training were all against it. The girls mastered me completely. I kept making horrible bloomers in my speech, and at each bloomer they howled in delight. That strange interlude worked permanent damage on my self-esteem.

Among the girls was one in particular, a lion among her fellows, a tomboy of such unshakable self-assurance that the others followed everywhere she led. She was my tormentor-in-chief, and I longed to summon the courage to turn on her worm-like and give her a hearty spanking. I half hated, half admired this particular girl, and all the time I was vividly conscious of her extreme prettiness. She was very little younger than myself, and I would have given much to stand well in her eyes.

I knew she thought me an amiable fool; I would rather she had thought me a tyrant.

One evening I was going as usual to the school to give my riot of a lesson. To do so, I had to pass through a clump of trees. Just as my way took me under a big beech, something heavy and human dropped on my back and nearly knocked me down. With thoughts of footpads in my mind, I swung my body instinctively and sent the thing flying.

I turned alertly. It was my pretty tormentor. She lay on the ground against the trunk of the beech and eyed me reproachfully.

I was angry, and subconsciously glad that I was angry enough to show it.

"You've gone too far this time!" I said furiously. "What do you mean by dropping on me like that?"

She got slowly to her feet and leaned against the trunk.

"You won't tell the Headmistress, will you?" she begged. "I heard you coming and thought it was someone else; so I hid in the tree. Then when I saw it was you, I jumped on you. I didn't hurt you, did I . . . ? You know, you hurt me when you flung me off like that. . . ."

I ignored this bait that would trap me into making the first apology.

"Why were you hiding in the tree, anyway?" I demanded.

"Because I didn't want to be seen, of course." She came closer and put her hand on my arm with a wheedling gesture. "I was breaking bounds. You won't tell the Headmistress, will you? I'm sorry I jumped on you."

At last that apology! The advantage was on my side. I looked down at her, and saw a very different person from the tomboy of the classrooms. The flaunting self-confidence was gone, and the cool insolence that kept her schoolmates in continual giggles. To me, her chief butt, she was being almost deprecating.

For a long time I looked down at her face, upturned to the moonlight. At that moment it was not the face of a schoolgirl. The entreaty in it was of maturity. She was beautiful.

"No," I said slowly. "I shan't tell your Headmistress."

She did not smile. She said again:

"I'm sorry I jumped on you. . . ."

My fiddle case dropped from me unheeded. I took her in my arms and kissed her. We were not boy and girl at that moment, but man and woman. We looked at one another. She took my face between her hands and kissed me; then she slipped away. A few yards distant she stopped.

"Tomorrow, after the class?" she whispered.

I was more than usually ineffective in my teaching that night; and my pupils, even without the presence of their ringleader, more than usually obstreperous. The following night I was worse still, and the girls must have been astonished at their leader's forbearance in not taking the customary advantage of my blunders. She was quiet as a mouse throughout the lesson, and did not once raise her eyes.

Under the tree we met again, and next day I confided in Mrs. Taylor that I had fallen passionately in love with one of my pupils and wanted to marry her.

She warned me against loosing the curb on my emotions. She pointed out that the girl came of a good family of some substance, and asked whether it was right for me to let the girl give up the comfortable background of her life for the makeshifts and insecurity that were all I could offer her. She protested how very young we both were, and how our feelings were liable to change.

It made no difference. I was stubborn as a mule. I had made up my mind, and with my young beloved I had made a pact. That night neither of us appeared at the music class. We were aboard a train bound for London.

VII

WHEN we were married, I took her to live in the caravan. My wife's temperament was just suited to the life—until it became monotonous. It was as Mrs. Taylor had warned me. The life I had to offer her was not enough to compensate for the life she had given up. Our case was the case of Basil's parents reversed. After the first few months, my wife was never wholly content with van life. The blood of house-dwellers was in her body, and she could not in her heart dissociate the idea of married life from the idea of a settled home. I could give her change, excitement, even adventure; but at bottom she was not of that tough breed of women for whom these things never pall.

These developments resolved themselves gradually, however. At first we were supremely happy. We were young and reckless and leaped to meet the hazard of life.

Among my friends was a youth who, although he was already something of a prodigy, would probably have been surprised to be told that his destiny was to be proclaimed by many good judges as the greatest English violinist of his generation. His name was Albert Sammons.

103

At the time Albert, though still a mere boy, was playing in the orchestra at the Savoy Theater, where, needless to say, the Gilbert and Sullivan operas were going very strongly indeed. As Albert had often to be absent owing to other engagements, I acted regularly as his deputy, until soon I was made a full member of the orchestra myself. Another member of the orchestra, comparatively obscure at the time as a composer, was Edward German.

From there I went to the Monico, then at the high tide of its celebrity. The great Monico himself was at the helm, and the restaurant had a distinguished clientele.

Monico had come to England some years before to seek his fortune in company with another man from his native Naples called Albano, who played the double-bass. When they landed they had very few pounds to their name. Fate decreed that the restaurateur should become a great success, while the musician did not. Monico, however, did not forget his friend, and, when he first introduced music into his restaurant, he made Albano leader of the orchestra.

As the band increased with the success of the restaurant, however, it became more and more inconvenient to have a double-bass player as leader, and the first violinist was elevated to that position. This man was an excellent musician, and it was a band of considerable quality when I joined. Most of its members were Italians, trained in famous conservatoires on the Continent, and I, not slow to learn, was initiated by them into many of the subtleties of my instrument, which I had missed in my more haphazard form of training. As the weeks passed, I kept on mastering the finer points of fiddling, and improved immensely.

Among us was one, a surly jealous fellow, with the mean ambitions of his kind. By a variety of means he set out to damage our leader in Monico's eyes. He worked one man off against the other, so that there was continual friction between the orchestra leader and the proprietor of the restaurant. The quality of the music did not deteriorate as a result, but the atmosphere was unpleasantly strained.

During the time I worked there, I did not allow myself to lose my rather eccentric individuality. In contrast to the uniform evening dress of the other musicians, I wore my favorite garb: checked trousers, a velvet jacket, and a garishly colored shirt. I wore no collar to my shirt, but sometimes I had a bright silk scarf knotted about my throat.

This peculiarity of mine was a source of continual distress to the conventionally-minded Monico. When he saw me arrive to play, he would wince and say to me pleadingly:

"You know, you dress"—an impotent gesture of the hands—"too *much*. *Eef* you please, a *leetle* more dress!"

And, curiously enough, I knew exactly what this rather mysterious statement was meant to convey.

The campaign against the orchestra leader had by now convinced Monico that his chief musician was a fourth-rate exponent of his art, while the latter was sure that his employer was an interfering fool without any knowledge of anything outside of food and cutlery. The upshot was an open row between them, a passionate vociferous affair in the traditional Neapolitan fashion, ending in the dismissal of the leader.

It seemed now as if the mischief-maker would get his desire, this being of course the vacant leadership. But Monico sprang a surprise. He appointed me. Perhaps he thought that my unconventional style of dressing would be less out of place if I were leader than if I continued among the rank and file.

For some time I was leader there; then I heard of a vacancy in the orchestra at the Hyde Park Hotel. At the time this orchestra was under the direction of Botticelli, who had left the position of Court Violinist at Madrid to take up the conductorship at the Hyde Park. He was one of the greatest violinists of the day, and I thought it would be a great chance to improve my own playing if I were under him. With this in mind, I left the Monico and went to the Hyde Park.

In addition, I used to do a great deal of deputizing at the Waldorf Hotel, which at this time had, under the leadership of Albert Sammons, a splendid orchestra.

Another great friend of mine, Philip Cathie, was

the leader and violin soloist of the Beecham Symphony Orchestra. At what was, I believe, the first of the Symphony Orchestra's concerts to be held at the Albert Hall, Cathie had a great success in the Mozart Concerto. On his way home, contrary to his usual practise of walking home from engagements, he took a cab. There was an accident, the cab turned over, and both of his legs were broken. Thus poor Cathie, at a vital point in his career, was put out of action for the whole season.

It happened that, the day after hearing of this vile piece of luck, I was playing at the Waldorf. Sammons, as ever, was in brilliant form, and, in playing the final movement of the Mendelssohn Concerto, took it at a great pace. It was a wonderful performance, and the applause went on and on after it.

In the midst of the cheering, a dapper gentleman with a pointed beard left his table and came across to Sammons.

"You played that passage much too fast," he said. "Don't you know the metronome mark for it?" and went on to say that the metronome mark was so and so.

Sammons looked round the Palm Court which was still ringing with applause and cries of "Encore!"

"They seem quite satisfied with the time I took," he remarked. "Evidently you are the only person here who knows the proper metronome mark."

The gentleman did not reply to that, but brought a card from his pocket and handed it to Sammons.

"I'd be glad if you'd call round and see me to-morrow," he said, and returned to his table.

I leaned forward.

"What was the argument about?" I asked Sammons.

"About my time. He was telling me the proper metronome for that last passage. He left his card."

I glanced at the card in his hand. It was inscribed, "Thomas Beecham."

We looked at one another, then across at the little bearded man, now sitting at his table again.

"He asked me to go and see him tomorrow," said Sammons.

"You'd better go," I retorted. "I heard yesterday that poor Philip Cathie broke both his legs in a cab accident. The Beecham Orchestra is without a leader at the moment."

Sure enough, when Sammons called on Beecham the following morning, he was offered the leadership of the Symphony Orchestra at the Albert Hall. Naturally, he accepted. And thus, because some London cabby had driven carelessly, was provided what was perhaps the most vital stepping-stone in the rise to fame of our greatest soloist.

That accident had its repercussions on my own career as well, for, on Sammons leaving the Waldorf, I was offered his place. At the Waldorf I remained for a considerable time; and then I joined

an orchestra under Julian Kandt, with whom I remained for a longer time still.

This orchestra was one of the first of the type
now called Viennese, Hungarian, Tzigane, Gypsy,
or what you will: a type with a very strong emotional tone, and very marked light and shade in the
values of their work. These bands were decisively
"popular" in their appeal, but they maintained a
consistently higher standard, and played better
music with better exposition, than most of the "popular" orchestras. They had also more dignity. I
believe that Kandt, for instance, was a product of
the East End of London, but he had perfect musical
manners.

I, myself, run a band at this moment which is on
the "Hungarian" lines, and I should be the last, for
that reason, to suggest that the old-time bands of
that type were better than those of the present day,
did I not sincerely believe it to be so. In my opinion men such as Kandt, Worms and Gottlieb were
finer interpreters of finer music of this type than
any conductor of the moment. I think that Kandt
was slightly the best of all, and I have played under
the three.

We were engaged to play at the Royal Yacht
Squadron Club at Cowes. We were very successful, and as a result received a command to perform
before King Edward and Queen Alexandra on the
royal yacht *Victoria and Albert*. We were tremen-

dously excited, and long hours of acute trepidation were spent over the preparation of our program.

We duly "came aboard" that lovely craft, and were met by an equerry who informed us that we must prepare to give our performance on deck, as His Majesty had expressed the wish to listen to us in the open air. We got ready, and presently the King appeared with a number of other gentlemen. He nodded to us, smiled, and bade us begin. We went through our program with anxious care. The King was particularly attracted by Boccherini's Minuet, and had us play it twice.

From almost the beginning, however, the fair breeze that was blowing had caused us some trouble by blowing our music about. It culminated in my music being blown off its stand and across the deck in the direction of the King. As it was fluttering past him, he shot out a foot with the dexterity of a center-forward and neatly trapped the errant sheet. Then, before I could retrieve it from the deck, he bent and picked it up. He handed it back to me with a smile, and suggested that we might give up the sunshine of the deck for the less draughty regions below.

Accordingly we did so, some of the crew attending to the removal of the piano. We had barely started again in the stateroom, when Queen Alexandra appeared. She seemed to be a little deaf, but passionately fond of music, particularly pianoforte music, and leaned on the piano top when our pianist gave a solo, with her body inclined slightly forward, as if in eagerness not to miss a note.

When the concert was over, King Edward took the instrument of one of our violinists and examined it curiously.

"That is five hundred years old, Your Majesty," said Kandt with what seemed to me profuse exaggeration.

"It is a beautiful instrument," said the King, and handed it back as though it were made of some substance so fragile that it might break under the light pressure of his hands.

"Where do you come from?" he asked one of us.

It happened that the man addressed knew more about music than geography; but realizing that the King was evidently misled by the "Viennese" in the title of the band, answered loyally:

"From Venice, like the rest of us, Your Majesty. We're all Viennese!"

I heard one of the gentlemen of the suite say to another: "By his accent, I should have said his native town was Camden!"

King Edward, with what must have been the skill of long practise, did not allow himself to smile.

Shortly afterwards, again with Kandt's orchestra, I had the privilege of playing before royalty. We were summed to Windsor to play at a concert in aid of some charity connected with the Castle. We had a most impressive audience. As well as the King and Queen, their eldest grandchildren, the present King Edward and Duke of York, both small boys, and Princess Mary, a still tinier girl, were there.

One of the royal boys, I remember, I think it was the Duke of York, seemed to be fascinated by my admittedly strange looks. At the close of the affair, he said to Kandt, indicating me:

"That gentleman looks like an artist."

Kandt answered that I was an artist.

"Not the sort of artist I mean!" was the reply.

It is a source of satisfaction that I was thus picked out from others for particular notice by a royal prince. There are compensations sometimes for being a queer-looking specimen!

At this time Kandt was being regularly engaged by the Westminster family for the brilliant functions they held in Eaton Hall in Cheshire. We were playing out there almost as much as we were playing in London.

The Duke of Westminster had a curious foible. Although quite a connoisseur of music, he pretended to be a complete Philistine regarding it, for at the time it was considered rather effeminate for a man to be too fond of the arts. In consequence, when he felt he had shown more than the proper amount of enthusiasm for any piece, he would try to cancel it out by picking up a bassoon, for instance, and saying, "That's a good 'cello," thus displaying ostentatiously an ignorance of music more in keeping with the existing standards of "good form."

The then Duchess, on the other hand, was an un-
repentant music lover, and herself possessed an unusually good mezzo-soprano voice. She was continually pressed to sing by her friends, but, being
of a somewhat temperamental disposition, could not
be prevailed upon to do so unless the atmosphere
was exactly "right." In case she did feel like singing, the organist from a local church, her favorite
accompanist, would appear at all her parties and
wait about, sometimes until the early hours of the
morning, in readiness to accompany the Duchess
through "Melisande in the Wood," which was her
most successful song and which she sang charmingly. On occasions when she would not sing, the
unfortunate organist would almost inevitably be
completely forgotten, and it was often the Duke
who would notice the poor man sitting about dole-
fully far on in the evening and genially give him
permission to go home.

There was a time when we of the band were also
forgotten, but in this case we were left playing, instead of waiting to play. We bravely rattled out
one waltz after another, and those who were dancing
to our music would give us such applause that, not
being our own masters, we had no option but to
strike up another immediately. The dancers were
performing their exercises in relays, but we were
performing ours without any rest. The sweat was
pouring down our anguished faces, but still they en-
cored. We had actually been playing non-stop for

two hours before old Mrs. Cornwallis-West, mother of these beautiful sisters the Duchess of Westminster and the Princess of Pless, noticed our plight and contrived a breathing-space for us instantly.

Among the most frequent of guests at Eaton Hall was the King of Spain. He was a gay, vital young man with an irrepressible, not to say boisterous, sense of humor. He and the Duke of Westminster were great friends.

It appeared that one night another of the guests, who lived in a big house nearby, was boasting of the burglar-proof character of his abode. The Duke disagreed about the infallibility of his guest's arrangements to keep out housebreakers, and had jokingly declared that those at Eaton Hall were much superior. The argument waxed, the guest explaining in detail all the precautions he had taken for the safety of his property, and ended with the Duke wagering that the other's house would be successfully broken into before Eaton Hall was.

All this transpired later, but we of the orchestra were by chance to be involved as spectators in the consequences of that bet.

After playing as usual at the Hall, we set off one night, or rather early morning, for Chester, where we were accustomed to stay in a certain hotel. Our brake had just set off down the drive when we heard a muffled crash from somewhere in front which sounded like a heavy collision. On coming to the lodge gates at the end of the drive, we discovered the origin of the sound.

A car stood with its crushed nose pressed against one of the gateposts. As we approached the wreck, two figures climbed out of one of the doors. Coming nearer, we recognized King Alphonso and the Duke of Westminster. They were laughing heartily. The driver of the brake, looking serious, pulled up to offer assistance, but the Duke, stifling his laughter, waved him on.

Afterwards, the story of the bet came out, possibly somewhat garbled, and with it that the King and the Duke, primed as they were with full information as to all the anti-burglar arrangements of the other party to the wager, had slipped away in the car we had seen at the gates in the middle of the party at Eaton Hall, driven to the burglar-proof house, and effectively burgled it. In their haste to return with the added triumph of bringing off the *coup* without being even missed from Eaton Hall, they had been undone by the somewhat primitive steering-gear of those early days of motoring, and had crashed into the gatepost.

VIII

PAINT AND MOTLEY

THESE were good days—but no better than other days. I had all the change for which my soul craved, and I was happy. Always in the background was the life of the caravan. During all my ups and downs and divers wanderings, I kept going back to live the old life of the road again. If in this book there should be more of the great world than of the road, there is no implication that the great world was the more important part of my life. It is only that the great world changes and flings new people and experiences to meet one, while the road is the more enduring and therefore the more unchanging. And, after all, one road is very much like another.

I left Kandt to lead the orchestra in the Theater Royal, Drury Lane. From that time on, I became one of the "profession." My blood became charged with the unique glamor of tinsel and footlights. It is a love which has endured to this day.

This does not necessarily mean that I left Kandt one day and went straight to a rehearsal at the "Lane" the day after. Between most of my occupations, and often while I was still engaged in one of them, I would go off with my own vagabond people again. I would buy and sell a horse or two, or doctor one, travel a while with the vans, then drop back quite naturally into the life of the London stage and music again.

I knew that I could meet good friends on the road, and good friends in London. There was Little Tich, who had a passion for golf and initiated me into its mysteries. We had rounds together regularly. There was a young agent called Lionel Powell, afterwards to become a famous impresario. I remember going with Powell to see Jem Mace, that figure of my father's early days. My father had said that the great boxer was a handsome young fellow, a typical English countryman; but to my eyes he was more like a dignified old Maori chief, with his brown face seamed and scarred in the battles of his tribes. He was certainly of the legendary gypsy type. Perhaps there is something in the legend after all. . . .

There was Arthur Collins, manager, at the time, of Drury Lane. There were Lawrence Irving and his brother, H.B. Sometimes, too, in company with Lawrence, I would meet his father, that titanic figure of the theater, Henry Irving, a lean ecclesiastical man with more of the student than the actor in his appearance and manner.

I remember Lawrence producing a play in which his wife, Mabel Hatton, was singing. In the middle of a rehearsal, Mabel Hatton stopped the orchestra, which I was conducting, and said:

"At the end of that song, I want the orchestra to come in with a burst."

"You mean a *crescendo,* I suppose," said Lawrence.

"I mean nothing of the sort," Mabel retorted. "A burst I mean, and a burst I want."

That settled it. Henceforward, in that theater a *crescendo* was a "burst."

They were a charming couple, and, after Lawrence's tragic death, it was from Mabel that I heard the circumstances of it. He had gone to Canada, while she had remained in England. At the conclusion of his tour, he cabled to her that he was coming home. She had then, she said, a presentiment of disaster, and cabled back asking him to postpone his crossing. Unhappily, he was not so easily persuaded as he had been over the matter of the "burst." He sailed on the boat he had already booked his berth upon. It went down in the St. Lawrence River—grim coincidence of names—and Lawrence Irving was drowned.

His name recalls one incident which, in its utter absurdity, shook my faith considerably in the probity of the British public and the critical ability of the British press.

At the time I was leader of the orchestra at the Queen's Theater. Now it so happened that, for the particular play that was running at the time, the music was restricted to entr'actes played during the intervals by the original octet of my father's invention: that is, my father, myself and my six brothers.

One day Lawrence Irving came to me and told me that a certain famous German composer of very modern music was to attend the performance that night. This celebrity had just composed a new work, not yet performed in this country, but which was hailed in America by the higher critics as a work of outstanding genius. It was an *Eastern Symphony*. He could get the score of it, and could we, without rehearsal, play it that evening?

Confident of our ability to do most things asked of an orchestra, I said easily that we could. After the first act that evening, the score was distributed among us, and an announcement was made from in front of the curtain. While the announcement was being made we were busy looking at the music, and even at that first glance it struck us as being rather peculiar. However, we had stout hearts, and, after half-a-dozen bored handclaps, we plunged into it.

There was a terrible blare of discord, followed by a sustained mowing and screeching like a bad-tempered wrangling between assorted members of the cat tribe. At first we thought we must all be out of tune, but we knew this could not be so. We were sure something had gone seriously wrong; and then we realized the truth. Nothing was wrong. We were playing the piece just as the composer had written it.

We had barely come to this astonishing knowledge, when things did begin to go wrong. The symphony was so lavishly without any sort of form, design or theme that it was impossible to tell by ear
whether one were playing the right note or not, and
in this connection our lack of rehearsal confounded
us. We lost our places. Half of us were at the
right bar, while the other half were spread over
four completely different bars. With moist brows
and white faces, we scraped and blew at our instruments, getting more entangled every moment, staring with eyes of horror at the incredible music in
front of us. Not that we had any real cause for
worry. The symphony sounded no worse after we
lost our places than before.

The playing slackened. It was touch and go
whether we stopped or not. Then my brother Fred
(better known as Fred Edgar of "Stanelli and Edgar"), who was playing the celeste, came forth in
the lull with a full strong tone, playing something
that never was on the score of the Eastern Symphony or any other published music. We relaxed a
little. It was a relief to abandon the Eastern Symphony for good. Bravely we followed him, and,
when he flagged in impromptu composition, another
of us carried on with some kind of extemporization.
As we were no longer looking at the music, we could
give each other cues by ferocious facial contortion.
As may be imagined, it sounded dreadful, but at
least we were unanimous in one key and kept to it,

which is more than can be said of the Eastern Symphony. I swear that our extemporization was better than the symphony. Events showed that others thought so as well.

For what seemed an age, we kept it up, and at last, with a conventional flourish, we finished. Exhausted, we drooped where we sat. I slunk shamefully from the conductor's stand. There was dead silence.

Then somebody began to clap—then another—then another. Half-a-dozen of them went on applauding determinedly. Gradually the rest of the audience responded. Presently the whole theater was cheering us ecstatically. I stared stupidly at my father. The applause went on. I returned to the conductor's stand and took a call. Half the stalls were on their feet, shouting for an encore. Little did they know what they were asking for!

Still they applauded. I took another bow. They shouted still for an encore. My father and brothers rose and bowed gravely. It seemed as if the ovation would never cease.

Then came the climax. Down the middle aisle between the stalls, a man in evening dress came striding, his hands outstretched and ecstasy on his face. He shook me fervidly by the hand.

"Thank you," he said. "Thank you! That is how I meant it to be played when I wrote it. It was wonderful. You have made me very happy."

It was the genius. I muttered something uneasily

and backed into the orchestra-well, bowing the while. The storm of cheering still went on while the grateful composer walked back to his seat and the curtain went up for the Second Act.

After the show, I saw Lawrence Irving.

"Well, it was a great success," he said. "The Lord knows why, but they loved it. What about playing it as an entr'acte for the rest of the week?"

"Never again in this life!" I said.

"Why not?"

I did not tell him.

Next morning our rendering of the "symphony" had quite a large press. Possibly due to the fame of the composer and the enthusiasm of the audience, very few critics had the temerity to throw brickbats at us (as we so richly deserved). On the contrary, there were many more bouquets, and some papers were really handsome in their praise. One weekly was especially handsome, indeed, and produced one phrase in particular which appealed to me powerfully. It called our interpretation of the symphony "a wonderful exposition of the European influence on the Asiatic mind." You may take that to mean what you like.

*   *   *

By now I was doing a great deal of conducting. In doing so, I did not allow myself to be restrained by the dignity usual in such a position. I would crouch on my heels and suddenly spring erect when

I wanted my orchestra to come in with a sudden crash. I would sway my body extravagantly from side to side. Sometimes I would leap high in the air. All of which sounds horribly showy, but it was intended, not for my own effect, but for what it could bring out of the orchestra. What is more, I found it succeeded.

Indeed I found proof of its success in rather amusing fashion. I went to a very exalted concert, at which a still more exalted conductor was on view. Imagine my surprise when I saw this great celebrity performing strange contortions very like my own. The longer I watched him, the more certain I became that he had seen me at work and was paying me the compliment of trying to duplicate my athletic feats. It was very flattering.

He went through each of my motions in turn. He crouched; he swayed; he sprang upright. I began to debate inwardly—with misgivings— whether he would essay that culminating leap in the air. A conductor's platform is a small arena for acrobatic exercises, and, whereas I had undergone hard athletic training since boyhood, this more famous conductor, being less in height and considerably more in girth than I, did not inspire confidence as a high-jumper.

Several times he made as if to take the jump, but each time he refrained at the last moment. I watched him, fascinated, deaf to the music. At last he did it. I felt at once rather pleased for myself and rather embarrassed for my distinguished disciple. He fell amid a terrific crash of brass.

I preened myself as I went home. There might be better conductors than I, but there couldn't be many better conductors who were better jumpers!

*   *   *

When I am old, and my shaking fingers cannot master the strings, I hope I shall have the sense to lock my fiddle in its case for good, or at least to play it only in some lonely spot far from anyone who might say, "I suppose he could play pretty well once." I do hope I shall have the ordinary common-sense not to play again in public after I have retired.

Being a charitable person, I like to think that stage folk, once stars of lesser or greater magnitude, make "come-backs" for no other reason than that they need the money. I should hate to think that they do so for the sake of applause and publicity, for the applause they generally get is mockery and the publicity ridicule.

A certain actor-manager, who had been a matinee idol of a decade earlier, made such a "come-back" while I was conductor at a London theater. He had been a good tenor singer in his day, and the handsomest man in London. His looks had suffered with the years, and like many men who have been unusually good-looking when young he looked older than he really was.

At the first rehearsal there were very few flutter-ings among the dovecotes of the female juveniles. His looks had failed him, and he never could act. There remained his voice. We struck up, and he began to sing.

He was fairly comfortable in the lower register, but when he tried even a moderately high note he broke on it. He could not even attempt the top notes. He raised an imperious hand and stopped us.

"There's something wrong with the pitch of that piano," he said. "It's sharp."

"Probably," I said, knowing full well that there was nothing wrong with the pitch.

"We'll take the song again half a tone down," he said.

We played the song again, half a tone down. He still couldn't get up to the high notes. There was a look of something like fear on his face.

"That piano's very sharp," he said angrily.

"Shall we take the song another half-tone down?" I asked.

"No, we'll scrap it for this rehearsal. I'm not in good voice tonight."

At the next rehearsal, I started off that song by transposing it two full tones down from the key in which the music was written. This time he got his top notes, though not without a marked *vibrato*. When he had finished singing, he said to me trium-phantly:

"Well, even with *that* piano, I took my B Natural all right.   My voice was a little rusty last time, that's all!"

It was pathetic.   If he had had any ear for pitch, he must have noticed the transposition immediately. As it was, all the rest of the cast and all of the orchestra knew that he was singing two tones lower than he thought he was—with dire effect on the unfortunates who had to sing with him.   On his part, he was pleased as Punch at the apparent continued quality of his voice.   The show went on with all the tenor's songs on that ridiculous key.   It was a signal failure.   Sometimes I wonder whether it would have been kinder to tell him from the start that his voice had gone completely and irrevocably.

*   *   *

Of the numbers of famous conductors under whose batons I have sat, I am inclined to think that Hans Richter was the greatest.   England, however, has no reason to fear comparison with any country nowadays while these three cavaliers, Sirs Thomas Beecham, Landon Ronald and Henry Wood are still at their best.   I think I should place them in that order of excellence.   Sir Henry Wood, however, is the most striking personality.   He always reminded me of one of the saltier kind of sea captains rather than a musician (referring to the man, of course, not the musician!).

While we were rehearsing once at the Queen's

Hall for one of the famous concerts, he pulled us up with a typical gesture of disgust.

"It sounds exactly like an orchestra playing outside a public house!" he declared.

There were loud cries of protest. Above the clamor, he shouted:

"I said *outside!*"

Such was the atmosphere at those rehearsals. They were good fun. During another one, Sir Henry, in making us play softly, dipped lower and lower until he was almost invisible behind the conductor's stand, only his head appearing at regular intervals as he dipped and rose rhythmically. Without warning, a coy clear voice rang out roguishly:

"*I* can see you, Henry!"

A rather curious experience befell me while I was directing the orchestra at Drury Lane. Everything in the orchestra-well was very old-fashioned, and there was one particular old chair which kept obtruding itself on my consciousness. In the middle of playing something, my attention would be drawn to it, and I would find myself staring at it. I tried to shut it out of my mind, but without success, and I used to give great amusement to the other members of the orchestra by fussing about with the chair, moving it from this place to that. Then one day, after staring at it frustratedly for a time, I turned it over; and there, on the lower side of the seat, I found the name of my grandfather carved.

I told my father about it, mentioning that I knew my grandfather had played in Drury Lane, and that this must have been his actual chair.

"More than that," he said. "Your grandfather dropped dead while playing in the Drury Lane orchestra. It must have been that very chair he died in."

I made further inquiries from old men connected with the theater, and discovered that my grandfather must indeed have died in that chair. I began to revise certain notions I had held till then regarding the metaphysical and the quality of being "fey." Certainly I never could look at that chair afterwards without an uncomfortable shiver down my back.

Generally speaking, I should say that stage folk are about the least inspiring class to spend a long evening with. They have to work so hard and for such long hours at their profession that few of them have time to develop any other side of their nature save that concerned with stage affairs. Shut in a theater during those hours of the day when the rest of the world is having its chief recreation, they have small opportunity to acquire more than one of the innumerable aspects of life. They talk easily enough—but always of the stage. A great event is not a great event save in its relation to the stage. A personage is not a personage save in the same relation. Their world is bounded by the backcloth, the footlights and the wings. For them, the stage

is all-sufficing. Broadway or Charing Cross Road
is the Capital of the Universe, depending on which
side of the Atlantic your act goes best.

It happens sometimes, however, that some rich
and strange figure emerges from among the uniform mass of theater folk. Such was Princess Ba-
rintinsky (otherwise known as Lydia Dvorska), bal-
lerina, actress, singer, and I know not what else besides. She was the most eccentric, bizarre figure
connected with the stage I have ever encountered.

At the time I met her, she was aging somewhat,
but was appearing at Drury Lane under Arthur
Collins's management. I and one of my brothers
were in the orchestra, and we had an opportunity
of watching her in full flight.

She had a habit, during rehearsals, of abruptly
inviting the complete company to lunch. But it was
well to be on one's guard when such invitations were
being distributed. The Princess was a vegetarian
of the most fanatical type. As she herself put it,
"I do not like people who eat flesh." Having collected about her the crowd of newcomers who were
as yet unacquainted with her foibles, she would sail
forth at their head to a nearby restaurant. Then,
having distributed her flattered and deferential followers about the place, with a grand manner all
her own, she would call for bananas and a cup of
malt all round. When faces fell, as well they might,
she would stare about her icily and remark peremptorily:

"I do not like people who eat flesh!"

I never heard of anyone who had the hardihood to wave away his bananas and malt and order an underdone steak. The Princess had the manner of a Mussolini, and appeared to think in much the same way. She could not forget she was a Princess, and we were obliged to pay the proper homage.

It has been said that punctuality is the politeness of princes; but Lydia appeared to think it wasn't much fun being a Princess unless one could turn up late whenever one wanted. She was never in time for anything, and we had interminable waits at rehearsals, ending at last when, with suitable regal grace, the Princess would sweep into the theater at the head of her perpetual court of attendants. While the actual show was in progress, Arthur Collins would go to her, after the call-boy had made several visits in vain, and say:

"Princess, your audience is waiting."

She would wave him aside with one of her inexpressibly imperial gestures.

"For me, they must go on waiting. I am a Princess."

But of all the strange things about her, the strangest was the Gypsy Club she founded at Hand Court. Here she kept what she called her Gypsy Court, chief among whom were myself and one of my brothers. We were, I imagine, the only members of the Court who had any claim to be called gypsies, the rest being made up of certain Latin members of the orchestra who were swarthy enough to pass as children of the black tents.

The most amusing things happened. Arranged upon an enormous divan whose shape suggested some Oriental throne, was the Princess. Grouped about her, looking suitably ferocious and hot-blooded, were the "gypsies." If any of her male guests approached her to speak to her, we would scowl at him murderously and, when he had retired again, one of us would fling himself on his stomach on the divan, seize the royal hand and kiss it. My brother, I remember, could be very effective in this scene.

We were, of course, properly dressed for our part, with property earrings and romantic clothes. From time to time we would nonchalantly scratch our heads or scrape our fingernails with property daggers. Occasionally, as a *pièce de résistance,* either my brother or one of the Italians—I was not very good at such effects—would perform the maneuver of flinging himself on the divan and kissing the Princess's hand, then whipping out his dagger and swearing to protect her against all dangers with his own life, if need be, to slaughter all her enemies and to carve up anyone who incurred her mildest displeasure.

My principal value in these proceedings, apart from my apt appearance, was to play strange wild airs at the right strange wild moments. The favorite was "Träumerai," and, each time the Princess made one of her theatrical speeches—which was one of her greatest delights—I would make the atmosphere for her beforehand by playing that piece.

I "attended" her once at a wonderful dinner she gave at the Russian New Year. The guests were all celebrities, and I remember chiefly Kreisler, Pavlova and Kyash. The great violinist played and both ballerinas danced. Kyash, I thought, was an even greater dancer than Pavlova. Inevitably I played "Träumerai," and the Princess inevitably made one of her long speeches. It was in English. Her accent was so strong that, as on the stage, hardly anybody could understand what she was saying. It was very impressive and emotional, however. The Gypsy Court went through its familiar routine, culminating in a series of wild "gypsy" dances. It was a sight to gladden the heaviest heart to see these sedentary Italians capering and perspiring with authentic abandon. It is sad to think that I shall never see the like again.

IX

THE ROADS OF IRELAND

I AM not good at remembering dates, but I think it must have been about 1908 or 1909 that I first decided to go to America. I like to believe that the fortune I meant to seek there was no more material than the wealth of experience.

In these days the strange phenomenon of Ellis Island had not appeared, but the Musicians' Federation formed a powerful trade union, and there was little chance of a foreign musician getting work there unless he joined the Federation, which meant becoming a naturalized American. I had a brother-in-law in the United States, however, who was some kind of executive on this union, and he promised to fake a membership for me if I came out.

My private affairs were not going pleasantly at the time. It is enough to say that my runaway marriage had been shaken into instability by its own impetuous career. I was morose and unhappy; and a voyage to America appealed as an escape from the monotonous circle of my thoughts. I let my brother-in-law know I was coming out, and booked a passage on the *Cedric*.

The liner was sailing from Liverpool. I sent my

luggage aboard beforehand, and went myself to Liverpool Docks in good time for the advertised time of sailing, which was 4 p.m.

On arriving there, however, I found a notice displayed on the landing stage to the effect that the time of sailing had been postponed from four o'clock until six. As it happened, this suited me very well, for my fiddle, which was the only piece of luggage I was carrying, needed a small repair which I had had no time to have done. This seemed a good chance of having it seen to. I left the docks for the center of the city, and had my instrument repaired at Rushworth and Draper's. I went back leisurely to the docks, arriving there about half-past five.

I strolled on to the landing stage, then abruptly broke into a run. The *Cedric* was being towed from her moorings and already there was about twenty feet of water between her hull and the quay. If I had been a champion long-jumper, I might have leaped the gap, by such a small margin had I missed her. As it was there was nothing to be done but watch the tugs take her farther and farther down the Mersey.

There were some officials of the shipping company about. I asked them if there was any possible method of getting aboard. I was told that my only chance was in going by train to Holyhead, crossing to Dublin, and going by train from Dublin to Cork. By this means, I might pick up the *Cedric* before she left Queenstown; but I was warned that there was only a small chance of doing so.

Naturally I was ready to clutch at any straw. Most of my worldly possessions, such as they were, were aboard the liner; my cousin would be expecting me in New York; and here I was stranded in Liverpool with nothing but my fiddle.

I took the first train to Holyhead and crossed to Dublin. In the small hours of the morning, I was carried southwest across Ireland and came to Cork on the heels of the dawn. On to Queenstown, and, with my fiddle case tucked under my arm like a rugby ball, I ran on to the quay. The *Cedric,* with the early morning light on her funnels and upperworks, was just standing out of Cork Harbor.

Back I went to Cork, cursing under my breath. With me went crowds of weeping mothers and sisters of emigrants to America, returning from seeing their sons and brothers off to the New World; for, in these days, Ireland was still shipping the best of her young manhood across the Atlantic, and the harrowing scenes of parting on that bitter quay at Queenstown were still to be witnessed.

I found myself outside Cork Cathedral, with the great doorway open before me like a pair of arms. I walked inside. The cathedral was empty, and it was dark after the bright sunshine; the high roof was all in shadows. I sat down and meditated, and my irritation at missing the liner for the second time seemed childish and unworthy. Feeling soothed and exalted above the cares of earth, I came out into the morning again.

The sunshine was glorious, and the air, with a tangy freshness in its smell, sparkled like the facets of a jewel. It was one of those vital mornings that instil their own vigorous life into one's blood. It was good to be alive and on the green face of Ireland. As I came out of the cathedral, a young priest passed me going in. He was a fresh-faced young man with a gay eye. As he passed me, he winked one of those sparkling eyes at me. He must have been caught up in the exuberance of the morning.

The wink cheered me more than anything. I thought of these female figures, sorrow-broken, who had been seeing their men sail away in that pearly sunshine. It was a tragic thought, but one which rallied me to find more cause for my own glumness than that which had occasioned it. I was young, the day was exquisite, the smell of the air was exciting, and I was in the South of Ireland. What more could one want of life? Shouldering my fiddle, I took the road to the west.

On the evening of that day I was on a road that wound away before me towards distant purple mountains. On my right was a wide bog and the valley all about me was a mass of wild flowers. As the flaming banners of the sunset were furling about the mountains ahead, I made out, through the cold glow of the dusk, a caravan at rest by the roadside and figures about it.

They were Irish gypsies. When they had talked to me and knew me for one of their own, I sat down among them. The fire was lit and the pot set over it. I shared their meal. They asked where I was journeying, and I said I was tramping towards Tralee. Did they know of any fairs where I might pick up something by fiddling?

They said they were themselves bound for some fair next morning in the neighborhood of Macroom, and invited me to come with them.

Next day I fiddled at the fair, and they seemed pleased with me, for they asked me to remain with them awhile. Among them were two who played the fiddle also, and one the harp, and they thought we should go well together.

The careless air of County Cork was in my blood by now, and I cared nothing about my lost luggage on the *Cedric*. I stayed with them and for six weeks wandered the roads of Ireland.

We were joined at one fair by a strange man. They called him Whispering Pat. I myself am as learned as most in the queer ways of horses, but never have I seen a man who could handle horses like Whispering Pat. He was extraordinarily gentle with the beasts, but could make them do exactly as he liked by whispering into their ears. One could never find out what or how he whispered, for the whispering was so quiet that a man's ears, so much less sensitive than a horse's, could not catch it, but the sound of it charmed them utterly.

Pat was known all over Ireland for his gift, and his services were always in demand, for by his art he could break the wildest horse. At the time large shipments of Argentine colts were arriving at Queenstown to be reared on the unique Irish grass. They were half-wild things, completely unbroken, and it was an almost impossible task to land the kicking, rearing animals from the boats.

Whispering Pat would be sent for. He would go up to the first horse and talk to it, caressing it. Then he would put his lips to its ear like a lover murmuring to his mistress. The horse would cease to roll its eyeballs and shiver and jump with terror. Like a pet spaniel, it would follow him down the gangway to the quay.

Poor Pat! He was too much of an Irishman to thrive placidly on his art. He rose up against authority and was executed during the "Troubles."

In these days before the Great War, however, there were few troubles in Ireland save the ancient ones of hunger and want. Even the County Cork, that storm center of rebellion, was peaceful as a still lake. Aimlessly and happily, I strayed from fair to fair, and all about me was the charm of Ireland; the charm of voices and kindliness and carelessness and gay fair-grounds and lonely cabins on quiet uplands.

By now our orchestra of vagrants was flourishing. A tinker girl sang to our playing one night and traveled with us thereafter. She had a lovely voice. Thinking it right that a larger audience should have the pleasure of listening to her singing, I tried to persuade her to go to London and form an act with me. But she would not leave her own people. Perhaps she was wise in her choice; but she would have been a great success in London.

From those who traveled with me I learnt a host of old airs and melodies, most of which had never been written down; and, even as I had learnt more about fiddling from the musicians from the Conservatoires, I learnt yet more about it from these wanderers over Ireland. They had a style all their own fitted especially for playing their country dance music, and they taught me their secrets of it, so that I could play jigs and reels with them at the fairs, using that strong upward stroke of the bow that is the kernel of the secret.

There came a time when I played at the Cork Palace, and so the thin end of the urban wedge was insinuated into my life again. Why I know not, for I had been happy in Ireland, I suddenly made up my mind to return to London. The men who had formed the "orchestra" with me wept and embraced me when I left. The next time I saw Ireland, men were being shot. . . .

*   *   *

Shortly after my return to England I collected an octet and made some recordings for the ummelodious gramophone of the day—or was it phonograph? Some time afterwards I had the pleasure of receiv-

ing a letter from Edison complimenting me on these
early records. I do not know whether the great in-
ventor was a critic of music or not, but I hope he
was, for I should hate to think that he was mistaking
me for the engineer responsible for the recording
arrangements and was applauding the mechanical
and not the artistic merits of the record!

Long years afterwards, I was passing a restaurant
in Amsterdam, when I heard one of these ancient
records being played within. I entered and told the
manager that the tune the gramophone was playing
was a particular favorite of mine. Wondering what
he would reply, I asked him who was playing it. I
had the faint hope that he might answer: "Why, that
is the great Petulengro and his incomparable octet!"
I had remembered Edison's letter.

What he did say was:

"Oh, it is some Hungarian band or other. I am
told they are all dead now, anyway. It is time we
threw away that record."

Oh, how I wished I had had Edison's letter on me
to show him . . . !

Now, some two years before these records were
made, I had been talking with Botticelli, the conductor with whom I had played at the Hyde Park
Hotel. The subject was South America. Botticelli
was firmly convinced that England was overcrowded
as far as musicians were concerned. A young man
must go abroad if he wanted to thrust himself to the
very first rank of celebrity. Brazil, he said, was a

musician's paradise. The Brazilians had become amazingly prosperous through the boom in rubber; they were passionately fond of music, but there were not enough good executants to go round. Even by playing in a café out there, a young man of talent could fill his pockets with milreis. He had been there himself, and he knew all the ropes. One could snatch fame and fortune in a night. They were building great concert halls and opera houses in all the towns.

I said promptly that the idea of going out there appealed to me strongly. He said he had a friend, an Italian, in Para to whom he would write about me. He was confident that his friend in Para would offer me an engagement immediately.

During the intervening two years I heard nothing more about Brazil. Shortly after the making of those poor overmentioned records, I returned to the Waldorf, and it was while I was there that the subject of Brazil reasserted itself. A letter from the Italian in Para reached me, couched in the most urgent terms, which offered me an engagement there at once and told me to sail by the first boat.

Not being acquainted with Brazil at the time, it struck me as curious that it should take two years to reply to a letter; but then I did not know the country, or the strange effect it has upon the energy of incomers from supposedly more vigorous nations. That knowledge I was to acquire very shortly.

As it fell out, there was a steamer sailing almost

there and then, just as though fate or the steamship company had arranged it specially to give me every inducement to follow my vagrant inclinations across the Atlantic. I flung some clean linen in a suitcase, grabbed it and my violin, and barely caught the boat. If this should meet the eye of Mr. Kneale Kelly, at present an ornament of the B.B.C. but then a young man of seventeen or so playing with me at the Waldorf, he will understand why I vanished so mysteriously in the middle of a week without a word to anybody.

X

THE SELVA

I SAILED on the Booth liner *Hilary*. When we called at Lisbon, the passengers witnessed a strange sight. A large gang of men were lined up on the quay ready to embark. They were dressed in the fashion of Portuguese peasants. Contrary to the usual Portuguese behavior, they stood in dead silence. They seemed sullen and frightened. Two or three other men shouted harshly at them when the time came for them to come aboard. Jostled and bellowed at by their overseers, they trooped up the gangway, their heads bent. They reminded me irresistibly of a picture by Vincent Van Gogh showing a file of convicts, more like machines than human beings, tramping round a prison courtyard.

Thinking they might be felons destined for some Portuguese version of France's Devil's Island, I asked a Portuguese passenger who had just come aboard who they were and where they were going. He told me they were, as I had thought, peasants from the interior of the country. They were going out to Brazil as workmen on the Madeira-Mamoré forest railway, then in process of construction. Each man contracted to work for a period of two years, and

143

the wages were high. This was all he could tell me, but the demeanor of the gang did not seem to me what one would expect in workmen earning high wages, and I was curious.

During the voyage, the gang was cooped up in a tiny space near the bows. They were debarred from straying on to the portions of the ship open to the other passengers and were forbidden to talk to them. They would play Portuguese folk-dances and dance with each other, but it appeared to me that their jollification was listless and without heart. Several times I tried to talk to one or two of them, but they spoke no English and their dialect was far beyond my few words' knowledge of Portuguese. As the voyage went on, their manner became still more listless and sullen. They ceased to have their dreary dances. They rarely talked to one another, and when they did so it was in fierce whispers.

As the voyage was nearing its end, I encountered a Brazilian passenger who was able both to speak English and to tell me something more about the strange silent company forward.

Those responsible for the great project of building the Madeira-Mamoré railway, it appeared, sent their agents across to Portugal at regular intervals to renew the depleted labor force in Brazil. The men were persuaded to leave their homes for a period of two years, on the inducement of big pay. But, when they arrived at their destination on the Upper Amazon, the conditions of climate and labor were so

THE SELVA   145

appalling that white men went down like flies. My informant declared that he knew it for a fact that hardly one in ten of those who went out ever came back, and that the fraction which did were the merest wrecks of men, useless for ever for manual labor. He said it was common, when a gang collected in Lisbon, for a whispered rumor about what lay ahead of them to go round among the peasants, probably circulated by those in the city who had seen other gangs go—and not come back.

This, apparently, was what had happened. A whisper at Lisbon, and they were already uneasy; then, as the days went by, and there had been time for brooding, the effect of that whisper increased. Like cattle for slaughter they were being shipped abroad; and, like beasts and men of low intellect, they knew instinctively that they were doomed.

We neared the Amazon mouth, that Gargantuan mouth waiting to swallow them up, and they grew more and more restive. When we were in sight of Para, one of them tried to jump overboard, though whether with the idea of suicide or of swimming to the inviting dark-green shore on our quarter I did not discover, and the seamen had a hard job to prevent him.

A squad of armed men was waiting on the quay when we docked, and came aboard immediately, where they stood on guard over the Portuguese. The latter by now were in a state of frenzy. Shouting hysterically, screaming and praying, they begged their guards to let them go back home. Like mad beasts they scrambled over one another to fight their way past the guards and were beaten back with rifle-butts. I never want to witness a more horrible sight.

With the other passengers, I went ashore. There was, of course, nothing I could do for the poor devils, but I felt illogically that I was denying my humanity in leaving them thus to their fate. Later I heard that another gang, which had worked out its sentence of two years, should have been taken aboard the *Hilary* on its return trip to Lisbon, but none came aboard . . . there was none to come. Only one man had survived the frightful conditions of the construction work and had been brought back —on a litter. He had died within sight of Para. If ever there was a great human achievement made at the cost of humanity, it was the Madeira-Mamoré forest railway.

*   *   *

Para was a grubby little town and seemed to have no buildings of any importance. The last was a matter for puzzlement. Where could be this restaurant called the Café da Monde whose orchestra I was to join?

The other passengers disappeared mysteriously. I was alone, it seemed, in an empty town. Nothing alive could be seen in the streets save a few sleeping dogs and a few vultures. At long last, after divers wanderings under the scorching sun, I came upon the inscription, "Café da Monde."

But the sign was over the dreariest and most dilapidated establishment one could imagine. It had not even doors to it. This was obviously not the place I was looking for. It must be named pretentiously after the great original, as one finds cafés in Soho with such grandiloquent names as the Savoy, the Ritz, the Trocadero. Cheered by this thought, it seemed to me certain that the folk who kept this place could direct me to the one I was looking for.

I passed through the doorless entrance into the shadowy interior. On the floor three men lay sleeping loudly under mosquito nets. I prodded the nearest. He opened one eye, screwed up his face in distaste and went to sleep again. I prodded him again, and he opened the same eye. He mumbled one word, "Siesta," and went to sleep for the second time.

The apparent emptiness of Para was explained. It was high noon, and everybody was asleep. Clearly it was no use searching farther until the *siesta* had snored itself out. I lay down beside my taciturn informant and went to sleep myself.

When I awoke, one of the three sleepers was sitting up scratching his head drowsily. We looked at one another.

"Speak English?" I asked.

"Sure I speak-a English," he replied. "What-a you want?"

"I want the Café da Monde."

"Here you have eet, den."

"I don't mean this one. I mean the big one."

"I don't-a understand. Dees ees da only one in Para."

So the dark notion that had been burgeoning in my mind was true. Here was my destination. I called upon my best recuperative powers and said:

"I am the new violinist here. Where is Signor Moroni?"

My interlocutor shook his head sadly.

"Ah, Signor Moroni. He 'as gone back to Eetaly."

Here was another blow. Moroni had been Botticelli's acquaintance who had sent for me.

"It doesn't matter," I said firmly. "I'm still the new violinist. Where are the rest of the orchestra?"

It turned out that the three sleepers were my new colleagues. The man I was speaking to played the accordion, while, of the other two, one played the mandolin and one the clarinet. All three were Italians, and it was not long before I heard from them the unhappy condition of their kind in this alien clime.

It appears that, up to a year or so previously, Brazil had enjoyed a virtual monopoly of the rubber-supply of the world. Then some enterprising Briton had taken some plants to England. Scientists had worked on them at Kew Gardens and had cultivated a variety so successfully that it had been disseminated over such torrid parts of the Empire as southern India and Malaya. There rubber had flourished exceedingly, and almost overnight Britain had snatched the control of the world rubber markets from the hands of Brazil.

While the boom was on, there were millionaires galore up and down the Amazon basin, and one of the symptoms of the boom had been, as Botticelli had told me, the demand for and prosperity of musicians in the country. My misfortune was that the glowing tales I had heard applied to the period before the boom exploded. By now it was already past. The Brazil of the time when Botticelli gave me his well-intentioned advice was a different land from the Brazil I found at the time I arrived there. The musicians, mostly Italians, who had flocked there to participate in the riches of the rubber harvest were intent only on getting back to Europe. Those who could afford to do so had already gone. It was only the unfortunates who could not raise the fare back who remained.

Of such were my three co-musicians. In them disappointment had given place to a kind of unremitting torpor of misery. They slept, drank, and ate, and beyond these they forbore to concern themselves. When I told them I was going to be their new violinist, they shrugged and made no objection. When the proprietor of the café appeared, he did the same. We all sat down and drank a colorless fiery spirit called *gasarsh,* or some such name, and waited for a customer.

Presently one or two Brazilians arrived and gave meager orders; then one or two more. We got out our instruments.

Our first number was a piece called "Fadoo Lira." We had barely started, when all the customers began to cry. By the time we had finished, they were sobbing heart-brokenly. We then cheered them up with "La Paloma," at which they sang and laughed with the tears still wet on their faces. But they called for "Fadoo" again, and we reduced them to tears again with a second dose. So it went on. The Brazilians are a volatile folk.

Our music, despite its effects, was very poor, as my hands, usually dry, on this occasion poured with perspiration, and with each tune I found increasing difficulty in stopping the notes. For all that, I was in a fairly happy frame of mind, for the proprietor had been lavish with the fierce liquor I had already been introduced to, and I was uplifted a certain distance above the minor cares of earth. Indeed I was so uplifted that, when I was presented at the conclusion of our performance with a bouquet of exotic flowers at the hands of a tough-looking Brazilian, I was able to accept the unexpected gift without showing the embarrassment I undoubtedly felt.

Next day I discovered the reason for my poor performance of the night before. My poor fiddle, an old English make, was rapidly succumbing to the heat of this alien climate. While I was playing the previous night, the glue had been gradually giving way, so that the head was rising with the tension of the strings, slackening the strings and making me play flat. The same tension from the head towards the tailpiece had dragged the bridge almost horizontal. No wonder I had been in difficulties!

With speedy adaptability to the customs of the country (not, perhaps, unconnected with the local firewater I had sampled the night before), I arose late, and it was afternoon before I set out to find someone able to repair my fiddle; and, in the course of doing so, I discovered an invaluable piece of information about Brazil—namely, that the real rulers of the country are children, *siestas,* saint-days, and vultures. There are, of course, governors and other dignitaries, but the proper apportioning of the duties and rights of citizenship are dictated by these four.

Not without difficulty, I found the shop of the musical instrument repairer. But that individual was still deep in his *siesta,* and I was told that he could not do any work before the evening. As I wanted to see the man himself and discuss glues which could resist intense heat, etc., I gave it up for the day and went and informed my employer at the Café da Monde that I should not be able to play that evening.

He was hurt and indignant.

"Plenty play—plenty money. No play—no money," he said with finality.

The arrangement did not suit me at all. I had had to pay my passage out, and had very little money left. I went back to the shop of the violin-repairer. It was closed for the night.

Next day I went back again. As I went, I noticed many people and a festive spirit abroad in the streets, but it was not until I arrived at the shop that I discovered the explanation. It was a saint-day, and the feast was being observed with the thoroughness typical of Brazilians on such occasions. Not even large bribes would induce my repairer of musical instruments to work. There was nothing to be done about it. I said some bad words in Romany to him, and left him to his holiday.

Having nothing better to do, I wandered about the town watching such of the festivities as could be seen in the streets. At that hour they seemed to consist principally of walking up and down.

I was wearing my accustomed checked trousers and velvet jacket. To my possibly warped mentality, there was no reason for discarding my familiar garb simply because I was in a land where most people wore white duck. The heat didn't worry me much, so I didn't alter my own habit of dressing, and that was that, so far as I was concerned.

The children of Para, however, had stricter ideas of what was right and proper, it appeared. They were free to amuse themselves as they liked that day, and I conveniently presented myself as a whole pantomime of free amusement. Where I went that day, a crowd of them followed me, roaring with derisive laughter and shouting I know not what after me.

I was perfectly agreeable that they should take their fun where they found it, and would gladly have performed a few acrobatic tricks to divert them. But they carried their enjoyment rather far. They pulled at my coat, jumping away as I turned, and now and again one of them would thrust his foot between mine from behind as I walked, trying to trip me. I began to get annoyed. At a corner a large soldier, black as coal, was standing, his rifle in hand and the bayonet set. With the civilized instinct that bids one seek out someone in a uniform when in distress, I approached the soldier and tried to enlist his aid in driving off the pack at my heels. But all he did was to roar with laughter at the antics of the pack.

Even as I was speaking, one boy came up behind me and wrenched for the twentieth time at the tails of my velvet jacket. I turned more sharply than he expected, and, before he could dodge away as before, I cuffed him.

Next instant, I got the shock of my life. The black soldier growled, lifted his rifle and lunged at me murderously. It was the narrowest of escapes. Only by good luck, bad aim, and a quick jerk to one side, did I avoid being bayoneted. As it was, the

steel blade cut a deep rent in my precious velvet
jacket.

A small crowd of adults had collected to watch
the pretty spectacle of the innocent children at play.
When the soldier growled, so did they. They sent
up a shout of execration as the soldier lunged at me,
but it was because the bayonet had not found its
proper mark in my stomach. They came towards
me, spread out as if to encircle me, screaming with
righteous anger and shaking their fists. The soldier
drew back his weapon for a second attempt.

It was not a time for standing upon the order of
one's going. I brushed aside those nearest and hurried up a handy side street. I did not run, and they
followed me in stops and starts, running after me
one moment and halting to debate my infamy the
next. It was an uncomfortable progress, and I
would dearly have liked to break into a sudden
sprint, feeling confident that I had the heels of them,
but I felt instinctively that to do so would be to
excite blood-lust unbearably. I continued to walk—
fast. . . .

Luckily, in my excursions to the shop of the in-
corruptible violin-repairer, I had improved my
geography of Para's streets, and I knew my way
home. They followed me all the way to my lodging,
and stood outside long after I had shut myself in,
arguing among themselves and continually looking
up at the windows. Then one of the irresistible
determining factors of Brazilian life came to my

aid, just as another had almost encompassed my downfall. The time for that excellent custom, that grand old institution—the *siesta*—arrived. With a few final sleepy growls the pack drew off to its repose. . . .

Thinking I had escaped the consequences of my evil deeds, I went to sleep as well, and dreamed that I was slaughtering a great crowd of children with a bayonet, killing them one after another along an interminable row. I tried desperately to stop myself, but my arms would not obey the summons of mind to drop the bayonet and be still. The harder I tried to stop my arms moving, the quicker I murdered the children. They dropped on one side of me in swathes, their faces expressionless. I awoke shuddering.

That evening I went to the café again and told the proprietor that I was still unable to play. He was very stern, but relaxed enough to offer me a meal on account of my wages. As I began to eat, I little knew that retribution for my sins was hastening upon me. A great revolting brute of a vulture came expectantly into the café, his talons flapping and scraping on the floorboards.

He came straight up to me and tried to dip his foul beak into my dinner. I already knew that vultures are considered of great value in these parts, comprising as they do an effective body of scavengers which doesn't need to be paid out of the taxpayers' money. They wandered freely in and out of people's houses to clean up scraps and refuse, and were welcome everywhere. Candidly, however, I thought this premature interest in the contents of my plate nothing but rank presumption. I snarled at the disgusting brute and shooed it away.

It surveyed me for a while with bleary eyes, then flopped across to my table again. With a sudden jerk of its scrawny neck, it dug its beak among my food.

I am ashamed to admit that I lost my temper. I cannot say what the proper etiquette is when a vulture insists on joining you for dinner, but I fear I was frankly inhospitable. I kicked my uninvited guest across the floor and out of the café door. I went further. I pursued it out into the street and kicked it until it rose on indolent wings and flapped away over the housetops.

I turned to reenter the café again, and there outside of it I saw the identical black soldier who had so nearly disemboweled me that morning. He was eyeing me with an expression of mingled fury and satisfaction. He arrested me on the spot and lugged me off to jail. It was a fine chance for further bayonet practise for him, so I suspect the reason for merely taking me to jail was that he hadn't his bayonet with him. Of that, however, I was not certain, so I made no effort to resist.

If they made any charge at the lockup, they took small trouble to make me understand it. They glared at me in angry distaste, like fastidious people in the presence of a lively piece of Stilton, and talked at a great pace among themselves, shouting at me every now and again.

Presently they flung me into a cell. It was very small and dark and smelt like a latrine. In the shadows I made out four pairs of incurious eyes staring at me, framed in strange animal faces ornamented with unkempt beards and hair as long as my own.

As my eyes became better accustomed to the fetid gloom, I discerned that the four men were lying on planks. There was no plank for me to lie on, and the floor was foul. I sat down on the end of the nearest plank, pushing its occupant's feet along to make room. He snarled something at me. Drawing my velvet jacket about my throat, I leaned back against the wall, inhaled the stench, and waited on sleep.

XI

WOOING OF AN ANACONDA

IT was not a nice jail. I should imagine that any self-respecting old lag used to the amenities of Dartmoor would have been scandalized by its provisions for hygiene, sanitation, comfort, and the rest. My cell-mates were not a sociable quartet. They had been incarcerated with one another for so long that they had become bored with each other's company and had passed the social stage of trying to hide their boredom. They simply did not talk to each other. They lay on their planks all day and dreamed of frail women. Life was one long *siesta* for them, and possibly life might have been a great deal worse.

By careful eking out of the few words of Portuguese I knew, but chiefly by gestures and miming, I discovered that my companions were serving sentences—apparently for the duration—for crimes ranging from patricide to criminal assault. It was difficult to coax any information out of them, for they had lost the habit of speech and had been translated by sheer boredom to an impersonal state so divorced from the little interests, joys and sorrows of the world that they had evidently lost all interest in the world. The resentment of the man who had been obliged to move his feet to let me sit down was symptomatic of their outlook. Inaction was a positive state with them and they were resigned to it. Unconsciously, the man who had objected to moving his feet had been objecting to my disturbance of the one thing that the world had left to him.

Apart from that one show of resentment, they did not worry me much. They were neither friendly nor unfriendly. They had accepted the taking away of their freedom. But for me, the loss of my freedom was perhaps the greatest torture I could endure. Upon the base of it was erected the complete structure of my life's philosophy. I had never allowed anything to fetter me—not greed, not convenience, not convention. I had, in my time, left pleasant places because they tempted me to settle there and forge my own fetters. To me, who could not bear for more than a certain time even the mild confinement of my own house, the three days that I spent in that Brazilian prison were agony indescribable.

Fortunately, I had all my small store of money on my person. I did not let my cell-mates know of it, for, with men like them, avarice is a quality which endures after better qualities have been dulled almost to nothingness by sustained misery; but I showed my possession to the guard, keeping my back to the four other prisoners as he peered through the bars. His eyes lit up and looked at mine with understanding. I knew he could be corrupted.

By the grace of Providence, I had some old letters

and envelopes and a stump of pencil in my pockets. I wrote a note explaining my case to Captain Stoker of the *Hilary* and begged his assistance.   Then, when an opportunity came of speaking to the guard without being overheard, I told him that I would give him so much to deliver the note to Captain Stoker. He would get so much beforehand, and considerably more when the captain actually appeared, and I warned him that, if he tried to outwit me by taking the money and not going near the *Hilary,* I would swallow the notes I had left.

He agreed to perform the mission, and I gave him my letter and his preliminary payment.   I waited two days, and nothing happened.   The suspense was dreadful.   Sunk in hopelessness, I became convinced either that the guard had cheated me, or that the *Hilary* had sailed before the note could be delivered.

Besides the loss of my freedom, that overwhelming misery, there were various lesser tribulations. There was the vermin, there was the dirt, above all there was the smell.   Eating there was like eating in a neglected public lavatory.   I retched with every bite I took, and was generally sick after every meal. With horrible rapidity I felt my body grow filthier and filthier.   I saw myself growing like these other vermin-ridden carcases in the cell.   I saw myself locked in with them until I died.

I had only one interest that helped to make that awful period endurable for me.   On the second day I had caught a little brown lizard which had been

basking on the one tiny window of the cell high up
on the wall. It happened that I had in my possession
an ivory piano key (I was accustomed to paint miniature portraits on little squares of ivory cut from
such and ordinarily carried one or two about with
me). I had also a penknife, for I had not been
searched on being brought to the jail, as I had fully
expected. Now I conceived the notion of carving a
tiny collar and chain for my lizard out of the piano
key, and, having nothing else to do, was getting along
famously at the job.

I had only the last few links of the chain to
fashion, when the cell-door was flung open on the
fourth day. I was motioned to follow the turnkey
outside. I came out blinking, and found myself
face to face with Captain Stoker. I think that, at
that moment, he was the finest sight I had ever seen.

Within a very short time I was free. The hot
heavy air of Para smelt as keen and fresh to me as a
North Sea breeze.

*   *   *

Indirectly, my spell of imprisonment led to my
entering a new trade. I became a collector of animals, insects and reptiles.

I had brought my lizard and his ivory halter with
me when I was set at liberty. Captain Stoker had
been very much taken with it, and before he sailed
he showed it to a lady who had been one of my
fellow-passengers on the *Hilary,* the daughter of the

Governor of Manaos. She promptly demanded to be able to buy it. I sold it to her for ten milreis.

Now it struck me that, if a Brazilian lady would give that sum for an ordinary lizard whose market value in Brazil would about equal that of a black beetle in England, simply because it had a chain on it, some other reptiles of rarer species thus decorated would fetch really good prices. Already I saw myself a captain of a brand-new industry. I would collect some more exotic fauna, garnish them with ivory chains and sell them for large sums. I thought it would be a titillating experience to be a millionnaire for a while.

In conversations I had had with men from the interior, I had heard tales of remarkable reptiles, fish and insects to be found in the thickest jungle. What particularly interested me was one of a giant anaconda of at least sixty feet which had been seen time and again. The Governor of Manaos himself had seen it in a tributary of the Negro River some fifty miles north of Manaos. The notion already born in my mind, of setting forth into the *selva* and acquiring the stock for my new business, became more and more attractive the more I thought about it.

While I was in the process of deliberating the matter, I was given further proof that there were possibilities in the trade of intensive naturalist. I caught a butterfly which had a transparent panel on each wing. Being completely without conscience in keeping with the best Romany tradition, as regards cheating a born *watler, captain,* or mug, I painted on each panel a monogram representing the initials of a man who had been my fellow-passenger on the *Hilary,* and who, incidentally, had had more tall tales to tell of the upper Amazon than any other.

When I showed him the wonder of nature, this George Washington showed not the least surprise. He had, he told me, seen millions of similar butterflies on the Madeira River. He was generous, however. He bought my specimen of this so common species for five milreis.

The blood of generations of my race who had existed mainly on twisting successive generations of *watlers* was now up with a vengeance. I caught a big spider, squeezed out its inside and filled it with sand; then I took four wings from two different butterflies and fixed them, two on each side, to the stuffed carcase of the spider. The result was extraordinarily impressive. I took it to the purchaser of the initialed butterfly.

"Have you ever seen anything like this before?" I asked triumphantly.

But he was not to be beaten.

"I've seen one or two up the Negro—not many, mark you, but one or two," he said.

"I thought it was something that had never been seen before," I observed, looking mightily disappointed.

"I've seen insects like it before, but I shouldn't

think many others have. I'll give you five milreis
for it."

And in such reprehensible fashion I collected the
small capital I needed for my venture. I bought
various nets and yards of wire. From my earliest
days I had been accustomed to trapping snakes and
birds and small animals with primitive tackle, and I
was bold enough to be ready to pit my gypsy lore
against the pitfalls and hazards of the Amazon jungle. In addition to my materials for contriving
snares, I bought an eight-chambered small-bore
target revolver. I should have bought something
heavier in the armament line to protect me against
dangerous animals, but I could not afford anything
more deadly than this revolver. As it transpired,
when the necessity of using it did occur, the weapon
failed to perform its proper function, owing to
rust. . . .

I was able to get a cheap passage on a flat-bottomed
boat which was going up the Amazon to collect
Brazil nuts. The distance by ocean liner from Para
to Manaos is about a thousand miles. The craft I
sailed on, however, was enabled by its light draught
to use various narrows and channels impossible for
a bigger vessel, and by this means the length of the
journey was shortened by at least two hundred miles.

Arriving in Manaos, I waited about the town for
a few days to get my bearings before venturing into
the forest. What a strange place it was in these
days! Perhaps more than any other, it had benefited

by the rubber boom. Now, more than any other, it had suffered from the sudden toppling of the industry. Here and there were magnificent public squares and streets laid out, the large planning of which had never been carried out. Some, almost completed, stood derelict with the jungle creeping inexorably about them. In others the buildings, half-finished, looked still more depressing. In some were only to be seen the sites of buildings, the buildings themselves having never been begun.

Of chief interest to me was the enormous opera house built by the millions the rubber boom had flung broadcast among the merchant princes of the town. It was magnificent, as lavish as the Albert Memorial. It was roofed with colored tiles. In this place opera had been produced on an unprecedented scale. The most expensive and celebrated singers and musicians had been brought over from distant Europe to insure that the jungle-city of Manaos should have nothing but the best, and plenty of that. Now it stood empty and silent, with the stucco already cracking on its flamboyant *façade*.

If one walked at noonday in the Manaos of that period, one saw heads appearing from every second balcony and window of certain districts of the town, and heard husky feminine voices calling invitations to one to come inside and find shelter from the midday sun. The men of wealth had gone from Manaos or lost their wealth, but the demi-mondaines remained because they had not the money to make their way to the cities of the coast through the jungle ringing them round.

The tragedy that hung over Manaos was epitomized in these poor wretches. They were nearly all foreigners—mostly German, Italian—yes, and English. What must have been their destiny in that alien town buried in the green hell of the *selva* is horrible to imagine. I spoke to some of the English girls, and when I did so in their native tongue, some of them burst into tears. They were not street-women. Practically every one had been, like myself, connected with the show business. They had come out in alleged dancing-troupes only to discover the real nature of their employment when they arrived and it was impossible to get back.

Meanwhile I was busy making inquiries about that most gigantic of anacondas of which I had heard in Para from the Governor of Manaos. There were rumors galore about it; but, by careful sifting of a variety of travelers' tales, I established it as fairly certain that the seat of these rumors was roughly in the district in which the Governor had said he had seen the reptile, namely on a tributary of the Rio Negro only fifty miles from Manaos. To my peculiar taste even the commonest grass-snake has an irresistible attraction. That fabulous anaconda called me to it with the sureness of a lodestone. I made ready to take my way up the Negro.

My preparations were not complicated. I already had the materials for fashioning my snares, and I had my second-hand revolver. I hired an Indian and two canoes at knock-down rates; and it happened that, just before I set off, I had further evidence of the existence of large snakes in the district, for my continual questionings about the reptiles brought to me a native with two enormous python skins which he offered me at the equivalent of about ten shillings. I did not accept the offer, because I meant to catch pythons just as big myself. With my own Indian, who, by the way, rejoiced in the pleasant name of Juan Agura Pura, I set forth on the quest which was to make me a millionaire. I am afraid I did not look the part of explorer. I was still wearing my checked trousers and velvet jacket.

The waters of the lower Amazon had been yellow —the color of dirty lentil soup. The main stream where the Madeira flowed into it had been a lovely clear blue. And now the Negro water—an abiding tribute to the accurate observation of those who had named the river—was black: black when one looked down into it, but like thin heather-honey when it dripped from one's oar-blade.

Where we could we used the waterways. Where they were impassable, we cut our way with machetes through jungle which, for the most part, looked very like the interior of the Palm House at Kew Gardens. As a rule, we found a clear space on which to pitch our camp at night, such little glades bearing a pleasant resemblance to a triangular English meadow.

On other nights we would sleep with an Indian

family in a palm and cane hut perched at the top of high poles; an arrangement which protected the family not only against wild animals of the non-climbing species, but also against a rise in the river of up to fifteen or sixteen feet. Such a rise, apparently, was not unheard of by any means.

During this and subsequent encounters with these savage folk, I was, for some reason, accepted without question and without suspicion. Perhaps they sensed in me something akin to their own wildness and alien to their more civilized overlords, the Portuguese Brazilians. They may even have taken me for one of their own blood, despite my weird and wonderful costume. Facially, there was certainly a marked family resemblance between myself and certain of my savage hosts!

How they could reconcile my brotherhood with my ignorance of their speech I do not know. Perhaps they took it for granted that I had been brought up in some distant city—and acquired my clothes there! Be that as it may, they appeared to look on me as one of themselves, which, apart from what it implies as regards my flair for adaptability, is not very much of a compliment. The Indians of the Amazon basin are, surely, along with the Bushmen of the Kalahari in South Africa, the most debased and utterly miserable of all human creatures. Indeed I have powerful doubt as to whether they are even human. And they treated me like a brother . . . !

I had one example of their attitude towards me

which was significant. When I gave it out *via* Juan
Agura Pura that I would pay money for any unusual animals, reptiles, etc., not a day passed without
a dozen or more Indians visiting my camp. Suddenly they ceased to come. Then up the river passed
a Government boat full of officers in brilliant uniform. Next day I saw the boat passing again, on its
way back. The day after that more Indians than
ever came swarming into my *hatch-o-tan*. I asked
Juan the reason for these comings and goings, and
he told me.

Evidently the Brazilian Government has some
kind of system whereby the Indians can be forced
to work collecting; but this can be done in theory
only. As soon as the Government officials are re-
ported in the district, every native for miles around
simply disappears into the jungle; hence their non-
appearance in my camp while the Government boat
was in the neighborhood. Taking it for granted that
I was of a different race from that which governed
them, they would work for me; for the Government
they would not work. A compliment? Yes—perhaps. . . .

In my dealings with them I had one invaluable
aid in the person of Juan. He spoke Portuguese, a
little English, and most of the local dialects. Without him at my elbow, my friendly overtures might
not have been so successful.

After eight days' traveling from Manaos, Juan
drew my attention to a place where nothing was

growing but a clump of sarsaparilla plants. Swamp was all around us, and this spot was the only dry patch near. About here, he said, was the home of the giant snakes. Among the sarsaparilla plants we pitched our camp—not without many protests and head-shakings from Juan—and here we were to remain for eight weeks.

We settled down to an unquiet sleep after a meal of dried squid, catfish and fried bananas. The sluggish air teemed with mosquitoes and voracious insects of all kinds, including beetles as big as sparrows. The heat was so overpowering that even one's mosquito-net was insufferable to wear.

During all these eight weeks I do not remember one bright day. Indeed, the days were so uniformly damp and overcast that, the heat apart, I was perpetually reminded of the Thames off the Isle of Dogs on a typical English November day.

The Government boat having come and gone, and the Indians having resumed their visits to my camp, I began to collect a miniature menagerie with great rapidity. I had quantities of snakes, lizards, gypsy-birds, and macaws, and a vast variety of strange insects. In addition I had several monkeys, tiny fellows little bigger than the marmoset and of a reddish-golden color.

These particular monkeys are charming little creatures, with very human faces and the best of manners, and make much more pleasant pets than the common Indian monkey usually to be seen in

England. For all that, I have only once seen a specimen of this species of Brazilian monkey in a zoo, which is all the more strange because they seem extraordinarily hardy. I afterwards kept one for myself out of my collection, and it lived two years in the English climate, eventually dying from exposure to a late spring frost.

There came a day when my collection began to assume alarming dimensions. Its quality, however, was not up to the standard of its quantity. I knew I could have procured most of my specimens without a great deal of trouble in the neighborhood of Para. I was impatient to capture something really worthwhile, and pressed the Indians through Juan to hunt out whatever clues were available to the whereabouts of the giant anaconda whose grotesque image was now ever before my eyes decked in as irresistible allurements as any lover's mistress. I asked of the Indians only that they would find the anaconda. I, with loving care, undertook to capture it alive by my own means.

They laughed among themselves at the preparations I was making for capture of the brute, but at the same time they were afraid I might succeed. They believed that, if I managed to catch this king of reptiles, the whole serpent tribe would hasten to the vicinity intent on revenge upon all human beings. They treated alligators and other such unpleasant creatures with as great contempt as we might a rat, but they had a wholesome respect for anacondas.

Juan himself was not immune to the general fear and superstition. One night he told me in all seriousness how the anacondas, when they grew to their full vast size, swam down the Amazon to its mouth and became sea-serpents: and if such a sea-serpent were to lift his head out of the water and breathe anywhere near a boat, the men aboard would suffocate and fall dead into the sea.

Where he had got hold of this tale I know not, but it bears an interesting resemblance to the tall yarns of old sailormen. Did the story come to him from some sailor, or did the old sailormen get the story from friendly Indians such as Juan?

While the Indians were unwillingly scouring the forest for traces of the reptile I was seeking, I myself was not idle. Every day I searched the riverbank for snake marks at spots which I could see were used as drinking places by nocturnal animals. Where alligators abounded, I did not trouble to look, for I was sure an anaconda would not share a pool with any other large water-dwelling creatures.

At last I found a place where there was a border of jelly-like mud some twenty feet wide between the river and the tangle of the jungle. Across this patch of mud a very large snake had left in unmistakable fashion his tracks to the water. My heart bounded with excitement. I was sure of it! I had found my monster!

I showed the marks to some of the Indians and demanded to know if they had been made by an ana-

conda. The Indians looked scared and shifty, and
their evasiveness was stronger backing of my own
conviction than any eager agreement could have
been. I wanted no more of them: if the anaconda
could be caught alive, I would catch it myself.

On either side of the tracks leading to the water, I
erected two poles some twenty-five feet apart. I
fixed a crossbar to the top of each pole, so that the
erection resembled a set of goalposts for football.
From the crossbar I hung scores of wire snares at
varying heights from the ground. These were not
made fast to the crossbar but were merely slung over
it, with their ends, which were tied to sticks of hard
wood, resting on it. I knew my wires were strong
enough to hold anything, but I was afraid that the
expected captive, in its struggles to escape, might
have its head severed from its body by the wires,
and it was for this reason that I had not lashed the
wires to the crossbar.

The idea behind the bundle of sticks was that, if
the captive managed to take to the water, I should
be able to trace his passage to his next landing-place
by the path of the sticks on the surface of the water;
whereas, if he took to the undergrowth, the sticks
would again leave his tracks plainly marked behind
him so that he could be followed to some place
where he could be entangled in a fishing-net I had
in readiness.

Now that the trap was well and truly set, I went
each day soon after dawn in a canoe and concealed

myself behind some thick vegetation at a spot some sixty or seventy yards from my snares. I thought it prudent to keep that distance and also to keep out of sight, for I thought it quite possible that, should a snake get caught in one of the wires and see me, he might well attack me instead of bolting, and I had no desire to make the too-intimate acquaintance of a sixty-foot anaconda until he had become thoroughly exhausted by dragging my sticks about.

From the spot where I waited in hiding, I could not see the snares themselves, but I had a clear view of the crossbar and the bundles of sticks. For day after day, I waited there staring at these bundles until they began to dance before my eyes.

When the something I was waiting for did happen, it was all so quiet and quick that it was difficult to believe that my straining eyes were not beginning to play more extravagant tricks with me. One morning, when daylight was not fully arrived, I saw a bundle of sticks jerk down from the crossbar—then another—then three or four at once. . . .

It was a moment of painful tensity. *Something* had taken my snares, but what? Although I had been careful to examine the banks on either side of my mud patch to make sure there were no alligators within a reasonable distance, this might be a stray one which had blundered into the nooses. It might even be a large animal which had wandered down to the river to drink.

But I thought it was neither of these. I had noticed particularly during my vigil that no large creature came to that spot on the bank—a circumstance which I attributed to the spot being the established stamping-ground (or sliding-ground!) of my anaconda. At that moment, I was already anticipating the thrill of triumph. I knew in my bones that it was the anaconda.

Trembling with excitement, I waited, my eyes fixed on the surface of the stream to see one of my bundles of sticks floating in the wake of the submerged monster. At any moment the great head and staring eyes of the monster itself might rise out of the black water. . . .

Nothing happened. There was no sign of my sticks. I waited five or six minutes, and then I could wait no longer. The stick had not floated out on to the stream: therefore my quarry must have taken to the jungle instead of the water.

This was all the better. It would be much easier and more convenient for me to track him through the undergrowth without tracking him across the water first. . . . But when I arrived at the mud patch and looked about for signs of his passage inland, there was not a sign to be seen either of his trail or of the sticks and snares which had been dislodged from my crossbar.

It was a mystery. He could not have taken to the water, for no sticks had floated out on the surface. Equally he could not have taken to the forest, for clearly no sticks had been dragged through it. . . .

I was beaten. In idle peevishness, I took one of the bundles of sticks remaining on the crossbar and flung it viciously into the river. The mystery resolved itself in an instant. The bundle sank like a stone. . . .

The wood I had used for my bundles was ironwood, for I knew it would not shred itself away if dragged for a long time through rough bush. But, until that moment, I had always believed that all wood floated on water. If I had had a normal well-balanced education, I should have known that certain kinds, such as ironwood, are heavier than water and sink in it.

It is a strange thought that, if I had had a more conventional schooling, I might today be the proud possessor of the largest reptile in captivity. . . .

XII

MUSICAL BOOKMAKING

SOME of the missing snares from the crossbar had been set at least two feet from the ground, and whatever had carried away these snares had taken to the water. Without a doubt my trap had caught an anaconda. For, moreover, it had not only slipped into the water, but it had swum underneath the surface, so that the only other creature which could possibly have carried away the snares would have been an alligator. An alligator, however, it could not have been, for even a giant of the species would have passed under snares two feet from the ground; while snakes, as I know from personal observation, often travel with their heads well elevated above ground level.

I did not set my trap again, for I had resigned myself to the fact that I had lost my anaconda for good. Being somewhat acquainted with the nature of snakes, I know them to be of the most delicately sensitive character. A snake which had once suffered the rude indignity of my snares would not return to the scene of such a humiliation. I had hurt, I am sure, my anaconda's feelings, and I could hardly expect him to pay me another call. It was a bitter moment when I resigned myself to never meeting him. I am certain we should have understood one another and been good friends.

I should like to make it clear to anyone thinking of hunting anacondas in the upper Amazon that I do not renounce my rights as regards this particular specimen. If one of them is found with a necklace of several lengths of wire about his throat—

Naturally, having so nearly acquired this monster as the pet to end pets, I did not immediately throw up the idea of capturing another of his kind. Indeed, I was keener than ever on getting hold of a snake worthy of the name. Circumstances, however, arranged it so that my hunting expedition came to an end very shortly after my imperfect education had thwarted my first attempt of this kind.

One day I was wandering alone in the forest searching for snake-spoors on the river bank. Suddenly I heard a whistle. I started in surprise. I had thought myself the only human being for miles (for I was far from my camp), but this was undoubtedly a human whistle. I stood quite still and waited. Again the whistle. Human though the sound was, I felt an instinctive uneasiness. I took a step forward. Next instant a bullet came spattering through the leaves, close to my head.

I dropped on my stomach and wriggled backwards into the undergrowth. I had my revolver with me, and I took it out and waited. Someone, for some reason, had tried to shoot me, and I knew that

the would-be murderer must show himself eventually if I but waited long enough.

I waited for a long time, then I saw him—an
Indian—and he came gliding through the leaves like
a ghost.

There was no point in telling a man who couldn't
understand me to stand and deliver. It was his life
or mine. I drew a bead on him and pulled the
trigger.

Nothing happened. Rust had jammed the barrel.
I tilted the weapon to examine it more closely—and
it went off. The bullet passed through the side of
my neck.

I had barely time to realize that I had wounded
myself before the Indian was tearing away through
the trees as quickly as he could move. I lay still,
not because my wound was so serious that I could
not move, but because I had glimpsed, as the Indian
ran among the trees, that he carried no firearm. The
whistle I had heard meant that there were two of
them—and it must be the other man who had the
weapon.

I stifled the flow of blood from my wound as best
I could with my silk neckerchief—and waited. I
must on no account show myself before the other
man did; and I had the impression that he would
give the first sign.

He did. Half-seen through the leaves of a sepucia
tree not thirty yards away something moved—something dark and with a sheen on it, like the shoulder

of a man. Cautiously I began to stalk him, crawling away to the left to take him on the flank. There was no point in rushing forward and taking a pot-shot at him, for my gun might or might not go off.

Moving with infinite care I worked round him. He must have known the woods and the difficult art of primitive hunting, and I could not take the smallest chance of letting him discover me. My gypsy training in woodcraft stood me in good stead. I succeeded in working right round behind him and to within a few yards of him, without being heard or smelt out.

Through the leaves I saw the dull shine of his skinny back. Thank Heaven he didn't look as if he could put up much of a fight, for I did not feel up to feats of strength. In his hand I saw an ancient breech-loading rifle. Poising myself, I made my jump. At the first sound, he started to dart away, but I descended on him while he was still only half-erect. He went down under me, and I had him in a wrestling grip.

I hauled him to his feet, holding him in the lock commonly used by policemen in restraining a recalcitrant drunk. He looked sullen but incurious; rather as, I should imagine, an old wag would look on being sentenced to one day's imprisonment for a trifling offense.

We did not talk. There was nothing to say. I marched him off.

That return to the camp was a nightmare. At

every step I grew weaker and weaker from the blood I had lost. The wound in my neck became more and more painful, and I felt every moment that I must faint. But I could not let myself do that. I knew that, if I were once to become unconscious, I should get short shrift from my prisoner.

As it happened, I did faint before I actually came into camp; but luck was on my side. I had got within sight and hearing of the camp before I collapsed. By that time I was reeling, and, had my prisoner but known, the tight grip I kept on him was effectively keeping me on my feet as well.

I saw my *hatch-o-tan* all in a blur before me. I tried to call out but I could not. I knew I could hold out no longer. Then I saw Juan. He gave one look of amazement, then came running towards us. The reaction set in. My grip loosened. There was a glimpse of dark flesh as my prisoner sprang away. I flung out my hand to stop him, missed and fell on my face. When Juan bent over me, I was already unconscious and the Indian had disappeared into the jungle.

. . . Why he should have wanted to shoot me I shall never know. I suppose robbery was the motive. Whenever I think over the incident, I try to persuade myself that one other person in the world besides myself liked my style of dressing, and that it was the theft of my unique jacket and trousers, ragged and frayed and filthy as they were after eight weeks in the jungle, that the Indian had in mind when he shot at me.

The wound was not serious, and I was out and about again in a couple of days. But the wound was dirty and would not heal. Some of my Indian friends doctored it with strange and evil-smelling remedies, but it soon became clear that it would be serious unless I moved with all haste to some spot where more civilized antiseptics were obtainable. Juan and I accordingly marshaled our menagerie, and we set out on the return journey to Manaos.

I stayed in Manaos only long enough to be thoroughly doctored, then took my collection of livestock down the river to Para. There I sold some of my specimens for fairly good prices, and was able to buy myself a passage on the *S.S. Ambrose* bound for Portugal and England. It seemed to me that there would be a still better market for my wares in Europe.

On the voyage home, my collection traveled as deck cargo; but the monkeys, small snakes, etc., I had in my cabin. This, of course, was strictly against all rules of the ship, but I had good friends in the ship's doctor and the purser, and things were "arranged." I do not think, however, that my cabin steward was ever wholly reconciled to the arrangement.

The captain must have had one of the greatest surprises of his life one day when, in making an unexpected round of the cabins, he entered mine and saw me, aided by the doctor and purser, hard at work stuffing food into temperamental snakes which had gone on hunger-strike, while various other strange creatures wandered at will about the floor and walls.

He was not amused. However, he agreed to allow things to go on as they were for the meantime, but insisted that I must unload my bedroom cargo at Lisbon. I did not particularly want to land in Lisbon, but on the other hand I did not mean to be parted from my room-mates. The consequence was that, when we docked at the Portuguese capital, I disembarked, taking with me not only the harmless creatures who had shared my cabin but those which had traveled on deck—the more spectacular pythons, boas, lizards, etc.

I remained in Lisbon for some days, and found a purchaser or two for my strange wares. While there, an extraordinary event took place. I was walking somewhere near the bull-ring, when a man detached himself from a mixed party on the opposite side of the road and came across to me. Without a word, he showed me a crude drawing of a bullock.

His nationality was written all over him.

"Are you looking for a butcher's shop?" I asked.

"No, we're looking for the bull-ring."

I told him how to find it.

"You're English," he said. "Come and meet my friends and have a drink."

He was taking me across to the group he had left

when I saw a lady in it who, it struck me immediately, bore a striking resemblance to someone I knew.
I was in the act of being introduced when I recognized her. . . . It was my wife!

I may really be forgiven for not recognizing her
immediately, for, although I had cabled her that I
was coming home on the *Ambrose,* I had no idea
that I should see her before we landed in England.
As it was, she had come across to Lisbon, where the
Ambrose made a long call, to intercept me there.

I am afraid that that unforgivable piece of ab-
sent-mindedness is not altogether forgotten. My wife
still declares that, if she had been an anaconda, I
would have rushed at her with shouts of delight!

*   *   *

I had not been long back in England before I became a bookmaker! It came about in this fashion.
I was back again in the orchestra at Drury Lane,
and it happened that for one stirring military scene
in the production then running a genuine Guards
band appeared and played genuine military band
music.

But the Guardsmen did not love their music
alone. Time and again during the show, half of
them would be absent at vital moments, and the
scene would suffer accordingly. It then transpired
that the bandsmen were absent on these occasions on
much more important business. They were running
round the corner in relays to place bets on horse-
races with a nearby bookmaker.

Despairing of ever persuading them that this was inconvenient, to put it mildly, I at last offered to collect their bets for them and pay them out the same odds as the bookmaker offered. It was a fatal move. Certainly I kept the Guards together in the theater, but in no time I found myself established once and for all as official bookmaker to the whole company, from the stage-manager to the third scene-shifter.

It was about this time that, along with J. H. Squire, I started the original Moss-Squire Octet, from which later descended the present Squire Celeste Octet. This took up more of my time, and, staggering under the load of bookmaking worries, I was glad to leave Drury Lane to play in Fred Karno's Karsino at Hampton Court.

But I left an enemy behind. A member of the orchestra put a certain sum on a certain horse before one of our matinees. Then, much later, when I was actually playing, he whispered to me that he wanted to cancel his bet on the first horse and put it on a second. I could neither hear the name of the second horse nor could I interrupt my playing to argue with him. I told him his original bet would have to stand and said no more about it.

The second horse turned up, however, and the man demanded to be paid his winnings. I refused to pay him anything, and the other members of the orchestra said I was in the right. But he would not have it so. He pestered me and pestered me, and always went away vowing vengeance.

On going to the Karsino I forgot about the matter. I was at last free of my bookmaking, and it was a great relief. But the ex-client did not forget. I came out into the gardens one evening after our performance, and was just lighting a cigarette, when I felt a crushing blow on my head. I went down, half-stunned, and through a shifting haze I saw my ex-client, his teeth bared ferociously, swinging a chair at me with murderous intent.

As I have said, I was half-stunned. He had "got in the first blow," and he had me helpless. As far as I was concerned, he could have bashed my head in, and I could not have stopped him. But help was at hand. J. H. Squire, that notable Welshman, had followed me out. He grappled with the man and hauled him off.

The situation, with its melodramatic suggestion of vendettas, was absurd in all conscience. But, had Jack Squire not appeared at that moment, it might have been more than melodramatic. It might have been tragic.

. . . Mentioning the Karsino reminds me of one ripe story about its founder, the one and only Fred Karno. Fred, like myself, had—shall we say?—an education of an individualistic character.

It had been decided to have a military band to play at the Karsino on Sundays, and Fred asked Squire and myself to tell him what we considered the best band available. We both agreed on that of the 2nd Life Guards.

He waved the suggestion aside contemptuously.

"No seconds for me!" he declared. "Nothing but the best. If we're to have these Life Guards, we'll have the 1st!"

* * *

In the days when I had played at the Waldorf, the pianist had been one Fred Russel. Subsequently this great friend of mine had got a berth as bandmaster on the *Mauretania,* then had settled in America.

It was not very long after the climax of the vendetta at the Karsino that I received a cable from Fred asking me to go immediately and fill a vacancy at the Knickerbocker Hotel in New York. There was little detailed information in the wire, but it was such an invitation as I could not resist. I cabled that I was coming, and booked a £10 passage on the *St. Louis* bound for New York. Remembering my last abortive attempt to make the trip, I was aboard hours before sailing time. . . .

My heart was alight with that sense of bold responsibility which comes from making decisions on the impulse of the moment. I felt myself free as air; and, when I saw the slender battlements of New York's skyline flung up boldly against the clouds, I cared not whether I had been wise or not in coming, nor that I had just ten dollars and no more in my pocket.

XIII

NEW YORK NIGHTMARE

THERE was no Ellis Island in those days just before the war, but America's hospitality to strangers arriving at her coast was not altogether unquestioning. One had to show proof that one was a person of a certain minimum of substance. It was not a task of much difficulty to get into the country, but one had to wait till one got past the officials on the dock before sampling one's first taste of true American hospitality.

When I landed I was wearing a magnificent coat, fur-lined with fur collar and cuffs, for which, in an expansive moment, I had paid £100. I was also wearing a top-hat. This strange *ensemble,* which suggests the stock costume of a villain in a Victorian melodrama, was considered to be just right for musicians at that time; I think the magnificence of one's clothes was meant to imply that one was immensely successful. The topper, incidentally, seemed to be the only one in New York while I was there: at any rate, I never saw another being worn in the streets.

Perhaps the officials at the dock were awed by my splendor; for they were rather hesitant when they asked me how much money I had with me, and, when I told them airily that it was probably about seven or eight hundred dollars (I was of course much too grand to know the exact amount), they accepted my statement hurriedly and did not ask me to prove it.

Fred Russel met me. We went into a saloon somewhere near Brooklyn Bridge, and I asked him about the Knickerbocker engagement.

"We're going to be a roaring success there," he said enthusiastically.

"How many have we in the orchestra?"

"Well," he said, not so enthusiastically this time, "as a matter of fact, there's just you and me at present. You see, we haven't actually got the job yet—but they've promised me an audition, and we're bound to get it, because I've got a pull with the management. And don't worry. We'll soon get the rest of the orchestra. Just come along with me tomorrow, and I'll show you how."

I looked down ruefully at my magnificent coat. I knew Fred. He had thought he had found something good and had sent for a friend to share it. I was not particularly put out by the different aspect of things as compared with that which I had expected when I sailed.

That night I slept at Fred's flat in Brooklyn, and next day he hurried me down to the docks again.

"We'll be just in time to meet the *Oceanic* coming

in," he explained. "I know all the musicians on the boats. Just wait. We'll soon get our band."

We waited while the passengers disembarked. Presently a man appeared on a gangway at the fore part of the liner.

"George!" Fred shouted.

The man came to meet us and greeted Fred boisterously.

"George is a 'cellist," Fred explained to me. "We've got a trio at any rate."

He then began spinning golden yarns to the new arrival, persuading him to jump his ship and join us. George objected that the Musicians' Union kept all foreigners shut out of jobs in the States, but Fred waved all his objections aside. In the end George gave in.

We tried to persuade some more of the *Oceanic's* orchestra who were known to Fred to join as well, but they balked at the uncertainty. Over lunch we summed up our resources. Fred had a little money but George had even less than my ten dollars. It was decided that we must get some job to keep us alive—"only till we can collect some more off the ships, and get the Knickerbocker engagement," as Fred put it.

We walked up Forty-second Street, the Charing Cross Road of New York. Nearing Times Square, we went into a German restaurant, the "Rascalla," where a band was playing, and ordered coffee.

With a grand manner, Fred demanded to see the manager. He came, bowing.

"I don't think much of your band," said Fred.

"I'm very sorry about that, sir."

"My friends and I are musicians. We have a first-class trio. We could do twice as well as this crowd."

The manager's manner changed noticeably. I thought he was considering having us thrown out. Instead he said:

"Go up there and play, then. If you got the goods, the job's yours."

George, of course, had his 'cello with him, and I had my fiddle. The manager ordered the original band to leave the platform. They did so, scowling at us. We took their places, tuned up, and burst into a waltz. It went down very well. We played an encore, and, when we had finished, the manager came to us and told us that we were hired. There and then, with no preliminaries, he sacked the old band. They used some lurid language as they left, which I must say seemed excusable under the circumstances. It was very rough on them. But they *were* a more than usually bad band. . . .

Our wages at the "Rascalla" were not particularly good, and we kept on looking about for something better. As it happened, our next move came about in somewhat unusual fashion. I wandered into the Central Hotel on Fourteenth Street and, between numbers, approached the conductor and asked him if there were any vacancies in the orchestra.

He gave me a curious look.

"Never conducted, have you?"

I told him of what experience I had had in that line. Without a word, he handed me his baton.

"What's this?" I asked.

"The job's yours. I'm fed up with this place. I want to go back to Kansas."

I took over the reins for the next number, at the conclusion of which my conductor-benefactor brought the manager up to me.

"I've been listening, and I guess you'll do," said the manager, which was his way of confirming the appointment.

It seemed that my luck was in, but it was not long before snags began to appear. On my second day there, three of the orchestra quit their jobs, giving no reason. I didn't mind that. I promptly installed Fred and George in two of the vacancies.

For a time all went well; then it leaked out that we three were not union men. The rest of the band picked up their instruments and walked out. The management was left with no alternative after that. The three alien survivors were sacked.

We were in a parlous state now, for we could get employment nowhere. Soon after landing I had tried to get in touch with my brother-in-law, who was a dignitary of the union, but he was away at some engagement on the Pacific coast. After the

Central Hotel débâcle I tried again to find him, but he was still unavailable at his New York address.

Matters grew worse. I sold my lovely coat (I had long since thrown the top-hat away), and that tided us over for a while. Meantime Fred was very busy about the docks. One by one he collected three more musicians, and then off one boat alone he collected four more. At last the Knickerbocker engagement was in sight!

We had a few rehearsals, but not nearly enough. In addition, not all the members of the collection were up to the standard we aimed at. We should have liked a little more time to polish up our company, but our empty stomachs would not wait on our art. We applied for and secured an audition. We played, and the expected took place. We were not engaged.

It was a sad blow, particularly for Fred. One by one, the band disintegrated and drifted off to seek various jobs in different parts of the city. Presently only the original three were left. Fred was in a pitiful state of sorrow and contrition.

Shortly afterwards the final blow fell. We were playing—how are the mighty fallen!—at an entertainment for the German poor of the city on Blackwells Island, when we were arrested for luring "seamen" to break their contracts by jumping their ships at New York. We were each fined five hundred dollars.

It was the last straw. Where could we possibly

raise that enormous sum . . . ? As a forlorn hope
I rang up my brother-in-law's New York address
—and, wonder of wonders, his voice answered me!

It was the turn of the tide. He lent us enough
to pay our fines, and, that being done, managed by
some wonderful and esoteric means to procure us
what appeared to be perfectly genuine memberships
in the all-powerful union. With that essential in
our favor, and with the list of introductions given
us by my brother-in-law, we were able to meet our
American rivals on equal terms.

Before very long we were installed serenely in the
Grand Hotel on Thirty-second Street. It was good
to be restored to the dignity of employment after
our recent humiliations. Pay was good and life was
placid—for a time. . . .

At the time there was in America a craze—which
I believe still flourishes there—for waiters of rather
eccentric persuasion. They were engaged, not for
their waiting propensities, but because of their ability to entertain. They did just enough waiting to
establish them as of that profession, leaving the rest
to their genuine brethren, and would abruptly leave
everything to the said brethren and break into a song
or dance or a series of handsprings. It was apparently highly diverting to the good American of the
day to see a waiter standing against the wall, decked
in his napkin and the sober raiment of his ostensible
calling, lustily giving forth a rollicking ballad.

Among these thinly disguised entertainers was a

young musical waiter with whom I became friendly and later shared rooms in Forty-second Street. He was something more than a musical waiter, for he was also a composer of popular music. He would thump away at the old piano in our rooms, creating pleasant little tunes, oddly attractive, in unfamiliar negro rhythms. Little did I know that I was witnessing the birth of ragtime, that youthful parent of jazz. It was more than that. It was the birth of a new generation of taste.

It was not long before the composer confided in me his hopes of success in the near future. Schirmer's, the firm of music publishers, had accepted two of his songs and were soon to publish them. The names of the songs were: "Yiddle on Your Fiddle" and "Alexander's Ragtime Band." The name of the young composer was Irving Berlin. . . .

But the calm days at the Central were running fast to a close. The trouble began when Alfred Shrubb, the British runner who had for years been without peer over half-a-dozen distances, was beaten in some race by an American. We Englishmen were promptly subjected to an unceasing flow of chaff, not only from our fellow-musicians, but from the whole staff, and even some of the guests who knew our nationality, as well.

We were carefully superior to it at first, waving aside all disparaging remarks about Shrubb with the retort that he was thirty-seven years of age at the time of the defeat. As the chaff went on uninterruptedly, however, our patriotism—until then, I am afraid, not very much awake—gradually shook off its drowsiness and bestirred itself feverishly. We argued loudly the superiority of everything British over everything American, and we rose to every bait set to trap us into indignation. I fear we began to lose our erstwhile popularity. . . .

Then another major event in the sporting world took place. Owen Moran, justly celebrated for a habit of concussing strong men with his good right fist, arrived in America from England to fight another exponent of the same art, Battling Nelson, the American champion.

As usual—and almost invariably with good reason—the American press was somewhat contemptuous of the chances of the British boxer. It was generally agreed beforehand that Battling Nelson would lay him low: or, to put it in the language of the country, "knock him for a row of home-runs." Nor were we exiles in the Central Hotel spared the anticipatory glee of our American work-mates.

The night of the fight came round. The unexpected happened. The fight was the exception to the rule which governs nine out of ten fights by British boxers in the United States. Moran not only defeated Nelson, but he duly "knocked him for a row of home-runs." Otherwise, he won by a knock-out.

The next day we could not be restrained. We turned upon the natives in the hotel all the cannons of chaff they had been firing at us ever since Shrubb's defeat. We crowed unbearably and unforgivably. By the time the evening came, we were very unpopular indeed.

Now fate conspired to seat at a table just beside the band's platform one of our more frequent customers whom we knew to be a reporter on one of the great daily papers of New York. During an interval in the playing, we had resumed our rubbing in of Owen Moran's victory. The other players were retorting as best they could with their old disparagements of Shrubb, when the newspaper reporter, who was indeed more than a little drunk, chipped in on the side of our antagonists.

The banter grew more and more extravagant. Then, while the reporter was in the act of delivering something mocking about Shrubb, a neat, broadshouldered man came walking nimbly up the center of the floor to the newspaperman's table. He shoved a newspaper under the latter's nose and pointed to a certain column.

"Did you write this?" he asked quietly.

I recognized the paper, and had read the column to which the newcomer was pointing. It was a rather facetious account of the Moran-Nelson fight, quoting Moran as having said: " 'H'over, yer—!' Hi says. Then Hi 'its 'im, an' h'over 'e goes."

The reporter looked at the report for a while without speaking, a smile of satisfaction on his face. He looked up at the newcomer.

"I did," he said.

"Good," replied the stranger expressionlessly. "I've been looking for you all over town. I just wanted to do this." And he smacked the reporter lightly across one cheek. "That's just so's you'll remember I don't talk like you said, and I don't say things like it, either. I'm Owen Moran."

The reporter was on his feet, his face livid. He let out a wild swing at Moran, who dodged it with ease, but made no effort to hit back.

That smack across the face had been the least violent in the world, but the management had not missed it. They singled out Moran as the technical aggressor, and began to converge on him from all sides of the restaurant, preparatory to throwing him out. They were almost on him, still self-containedly dodging the reporter's swipes and making no effort to retaliate, when one of the three English musicians gave a wild yell. He leaped down from the platform, flung himself in front of the phalanx of waiters and defied them to touch a hair of his countryman's hard head. The patriotism of the other Englishman and myself was now at furnace-heat. We too sprang down into the crowd and shouted our defiance.

Within half-a-second a superb scuffle was taking place all over the restaurant. Swamped under the full weight of a solid ton of waiters, we rolled and wriggled and heaved. Shouting patriotic slogans, we were dragged across the floor in that maneuver known to America as "the bum's rush." A little later, and we were lying on our spines on the pavement outside the hotel. A little later still, and our instruments came flying out after us. Owen Moran, be it noted, walked out with his restrained dignity still unruffled, and there was none to question his right to that more honorable mode of exit.

We picked ourselves and our instruments up, and beat the dust from our trouser-seats. It had been an absurd affair, but a gloriously absurd one. Filled with a lunatic exhilaration, we rubbed our bones and limped off to celebrate. We were ridiculously pleased with ourselves. Our heads were bloody but unbowed.

I believe the customers and waiters at the hotel enjoyed that gay fracas as much as we did, but that I never found out. The Grand Hotel did not see us again.

*   *   *

Not very long afterwards our "goodly company" was split up. George and Fred, probably as a result of the fermentation of their hidden patriotism on the night of our horizontal departure from the Grand Hotel, developed an acute attack of homesickness, and took ship for England; while I, after my inconsequent fashion, became a trick rider in a traveling circus.

This last came about quite simply. I saw that Ginet's Circus was appearing at a vaudeville theater downtown, and one morning when I was in the neighborhood, I wandered into the theater and fell into conversation with some of the circus hands. They were American gypsies, very different folk from the English breed; so different, in fact, that I did not tell them I was a Romany. I doubt if it would have meant much to them if I had mentioned it.

In the ring some of the acrobats were practising handsprings and double somersaults, and a girl was exercising a pony by riding it round and round. The rider pulled up just beside the group with whom I was talking, and I patted the pony.

"It's hard work this," said the girl. "This darned mare's been out of work so long that she's forgotten the way to trot."

"How would you like me to trot her round a couple of times for you?" I asked.

"You're welcome, if you can make her move," retorted the girl.

She dismounted, and I swung up on the bare back of the pony. Once I got her moving she trotted very prettily, but she was lazy and I had to work to keep her going. I kept her at it, however, and once she found out that she couldn't play horse tricks with me, she went without having to be urged to it. It was pleasant to feel a mount between my knees again, but it was dull work simply going round and round the ring. To vary the monotony of it, and also perhaps to show off before the onlookers, I began to do some fancy riding. I stood erect on her back, and turned facing her tail and twisted my body into several unbecoming attitudes.

Presently I got tired, dismounted and handed the reins back to the girl who had been riding the pony in the first place. I gave the pony a pat on the neck and asked:

"What's her name?"

"Polly," answered a man who had just joined the group. Then sharply: "What's yours?"

"Why do you want to know?" I asked in return.

"Because we ain't got an equestrian act just now. The girl that used to do it has gone and married a butter-and-egg man in Arkansas. You in the business?"

"I'm a violinist."

He raised his eyebrows.

"Couldn't play your fiddle on horseback, could you?"

"I could try," I answered.

Strangely enough, I did not find it too difficult. I brought my violin and made the round of the ring once or twice, playing erect on Polly's back.

"Not bad," said the man who had first made the suggestion. "You'll need to train a bit, though."

And I became a circus rider. In company with Ginet's Circus, I wandered from one vaudeville theater to another (for it was the winter season, and playing under canvas was out of the question) in New York, Philadelphia, Boston and Newark.

Strangely enough, it was rather dull. I, at least,

was quickly bored with the life. My act, too, was not one in which one could take much interest. I am passionately fond of riding, and passionately fond of music, but in combination both of them suffered. In addition, Polly was a dour beast and slacked at every opportunity, so that, instead of keeping up a steady trot, she would move in a devilish mixture of walks and jog-trots which had a lamentable effect on both my balance and my playing. When the chance presented itself of taking another job, I seized it gladly.

The new engagement was at Churchill's on Sixth Avenue, a restaurant known to New Yorkers as "a high-class joint." A famous artist named Gypsy Rigo had been performing there as an "eccentric fiddler" with such success that the management were eager to get hold of another turn that was almost exactly on Rigo's lines. They made up their minds very quickly that they would engage me as the celebrity's successor. Perhaps they thought that a fiddler who had, for seven weeks, been scraping away while standing on the back of a moving pony was quite eccentric enough for their purpose.

From the first, the "high-class" nature of the establishment was impressed on my notice. The habitués looked for an entertainment which might be sophisticated, but must always be refined. Many Europeans have noted with interest the American's inclination to enshrine his womenfolk on a pedestal of sweetness and purity, high above the common little faults of humanity. According to every American, women in the mass may be frail and sinful creatures, but his "own little woman" is always so spiritual and virtuous that it seems naughty even to mention her name in male company. Every American believes that there are two kinds of women—bad and good. The bad are to be discussed and treated as may be; the good always with sober reverence. The *motif* of my act at Churchill's had, as I understood it, to be adjusted so as not to jar on this native conviction.

I had to make a two minutes' appearance every half-hour from twelve noon until one in the morning. During this appearance, I played all the time, wandering among the tables, but I had to elaborate the act as well. Sometimes I would do a fall and go on playing on my back. Sometimes I would do a few mild acrobatics. Sometimes I would dance. Sometimes I would crawl under tables. Sometimes I would take little rides on waiters' trolleys.

Such variations of straightforward fiddling for only two minutes at a time does not, perhaps, seem to call for any great strain. But my problem lay in the fact that I must produce a brand-new caper every day. Not only that, but, appearing every half-hour, I could not do the same stunt two half-hours running. Patrons did not come and go as quickly as that.

For the first few weeks I had little difficulty in inventing two or three new tricks every day, but after that my invention began to flag. Sometimes I would come on for my turn without an idea in my head of what I was going to do; then my eye would catch a chair in a conspicuous position and I would curl up on it and apparently go to sleep.

The strain was cruel. I was having quite a success and appeared to be carrying on the tradition established by Gypsy Rigo satisfactorily. The management raised my salary, and raised it again. But I would lie awake at night wondering what act I should put on next day.

Gradually I began to crack under the strain. I fell into a strange melancholy state of mind and could neither sleep nor eat. Every time I appeared at Churchill's I became more and more conscious of my staleness. Although the applause was as loud as ever, I became convinced that it was ironic, that I must be making a pathetic exhibition of myself.

On one occasion only did I come up against the "not before the ladies" complex of the American man. I came on to the floor, wondering what on earth I could do as an original stunt. My attention was drawn to a young man and woman sitting at a table in a prominent position. There was a magnum of champagne on the table, which may have accounted for the fact that they were being rather noisy. On an impulse I strayed up beside them and, bending as I played, tapped the girl lightly on the shoulder. She turned to face me, laughing; but her cavalier, who appeared to have had more wine than she, was not inclined to take my action so well. She was apparently his wife or *fiancée,* and one does not tap with a fiddle-bow beings who are fashioned and contrived for nothing less than the rapt reverence of every true gentleman.

In a voice half-choked with rage he growled something at me. I was about to dance away when, without warning, he grabbed the champagne bottle by the neck and brought it down on my head.

The chief damage done was, I think, to my attacker's coat-sleeve, for the champagne poured over it in a bubbling cataract; but my head suffered as well. I reeled away and nearly fell—but not quite. Recovering myself, I picked up the thread of my playing, and, cutting my two minutes rather short, made my exit.

I sat in my dressing-room rubbing the bump on my head and staring in front of me dully. I simply couldn't understand how I had let myself be struck like that and accepted the blow in such despicably resigned fashion. It was completely at variance with the usual urge of my nature, yet I had made not the slightest attempt to retaliate. There was something seriously wrong with me. . . .

As my difficulties in finding fresh "business" for my act increased, so did the uneasy numb state of my mind intensify. With the people at Churchill's I acquired the reputation of being definitely "queer."

I began to do strange things. I stopped going back to my lodgings, or to bed at all, knowing that I should not sleep. I gave no notice at my lodgings: I simply stopped going home after my work. For weeks I did not change my clothes, both appearing at Churchill's and wandering about the streets hatless, dressed in a black silk shirt and the checked trousers and velvet jacket for which my weakness remained. I looked on the world through dull, incurious eyes. When I tried to think out any problem my brain would revolve round it sluggishly for a while, then shoot away frighteningly at fiery speed on some inconsequent tangent. The fact was that I was suffering from a serious nervous breakdown.

Every night—or rather early morning—when I left work, I went to Madison Square Garden to watch the six-day bicycle races. The public had shown little interest in these races when they had been started in the first place, but the press had run a series of furious articles couched in language of horrified indignation which condemned the races as "inhuman," saying that it was barbarous cruelty to subject the cyclists to the strain demanded of them in such races. The immediate result of which campaign was to pack the Garden night after night.

I would go there and stay until late next morning. There was something in the endless circling of the riders that fascinated me. It was like the bewildered rotation of my own mind. Round and round they would go, and I would sit watching them dully and uninterestedly. The ceaseless repeated motion, regular as the days and the seasons, soothed me and fascinated me as a baby is fascinated by the ticking of a watch.

The atmosphere was a strange one—hectic and yet restrained. Most of the spectators were folk who were trying to keep alive the fag-end of a gay evening. They were bored to death and wanted nothing better than to go home to their beds, but could not bring themselves to face the fact that the convivial evening had expired in weariness.

While the race went on its customary eventful course, they slept. Then, at long intervals, there would be a spurt. The riders kept going at a certain pace, cycling in a bunch, but once a particular rider showed signs of exhaustion and allowed himself to drop a few yards behind the others, the bunch would increase the pace in an attempt to leave him behind and lap him. Once a rider was lapped, he was virtually finished for the race, for the lapping maneuver had only been possible owing to his exhausted state and he could not hope to make up the distance lost.

On such occasions when the bunch, seeing one of their number ready to faint, would suddenly crack on sail, the spectators would wake up, and the whole arena would become animated in a moment. The spectators would jump to their feet and yell out: "Oh, you Harry, show your speed!" or, "Atta Ed! Make those wheels go round!" The vendors of ice

cream and popcorn and peanuts in their white
jackets would shake off their somnolence and shout
their wares.

While the unfortunate cyclist who was being left
behind was able to flog his weary muscles to the
extent of keeping up with the rest, pandemonium
would prevail. Then, as he fell farther behind and
the others came round to lap him, the uproar would
be switched off. The spectators, looking jaded once
more, would munch their popcorn listlessly, and
presently go off to sleep again, and the comfit-sellers
would drop into vacant seats, their chins on their
breasts.

At Churchill's, I had spells of irritability and
there was a series of stupid quarrels and differences
between myself and the management. But my act
was still popular, and they continued to pay me high
wages. Living as I was chiefly on popcorn-and-
honey and having no lodging to pay for, I spent
very little money. When I received my salary, I
would stow it away somewhere about my person and
think no more of it. During these fitful nights at
Madison Square Garden, I was carrying thousands
of dollars about with me, and had actually large
sums in dollar-bills buttoned up in the wide sleeves
of my black shirt.

As the strain went on unrelaxed, my condition
grew more and more abnormal. Sometimes, while
the riders whirled round and round beneath me at

the Garden I would sleep, but not for long. My
brain felt as if its machinery was entangled with
clots of wool. Of one thing only I thought con-
secutively—the necessity of formulating some fresh
stunt for my performance at Churchill's—and the
difficulty of concentrating my mind upon that kept
increasing.

Then, one day on my way to work, I wandered
down in the direction of the docks. At the quay a
liner was moored, with steam up. I recognized her.
She was the *Campania*. Immediately I thought of
Liverpool. And then, for the first time for many
weeks, I thought of England. Abruptly, ill and
dazed as I was, I knew that I wanted nothing more
than to get home.

I pushed my way through the crowd of people
who thronged the quayside waving to their friends
aboard. I found a seaman at the foot of one of the
gangways.

"When does she sail?" I asked him.

"Twelve o'clock."

It was just 11.50.

"Can I get a passage?"

"I don't know," he said doubtfully. "You'd better come and see the purser."

I followed him aboard, and he took me to the
purser.

"Am I too late to get a passage to England?" I
asked.

The purser gave my clothes and wild looks an expressive glance.

"We've a berth vacant, if you've the money to pay for it," he said.

I dug a hand into the breast of my shirt and brought out a handful of greenbacks.

XIV

THE PASSING OF ARTHUR

A FROCK COAT, which at a remote date was worn by King George, is now—or was until recently—being worn by a comedian in a comic sketch. This remarkable example of the vicissitudes to which such a garment is liable, is explained thus.

While I was in America, I met a man who had been his late Majesty's valet, and who possessed, after the fashion of valets, a number of articles of clothing which had been given him by his late master; among them a magnificent specimen of that most respectable of garments, this royal frock coat.

There came a time when I had a whim to possess a frock coat and don the garb if not the attribute of respectability, and I bought King George's coat from the valet.

After my return to England, I lent it to my brother, Fred Edgar, for some theatrical purpose, and, since frock coats had by then gone out of fashion, did not ask for it back. Only recently Fred in turn presented it to Wilkie Bard, who wanted something suitably antique to give him mock-dignity in a humorous sketch he was putting on. Thus, then,

did the mantle of greatness fall upon the shoulders
of the jester.

I am reminded of this queer life-story of a coat
by the fact that, along with my fiddle, it was the
only luggage I brought aboard the *Campania* when
I sailed on her.

Often I have wondered what induced that purser
to give me a passage. I had appeared but a few
moments before sailing-time with no more luggage
than I could carry, looking obviously abnormal and
distrait, unkempt and dirty, and wearing outlandish
clothes. All of which, combined with my long
black hair, swarthy face and earrings, must have
given me a notably unsavory appearance. I might
have been taken, with equal excuse, for an escaped
lunatic or a murderer on the run. I suppose the fact
that I showed I was not lacking in the money for
my passage had something to do with his accept-
ance of me; but I know that, had I been in the purser's place, that circumstance would have made me
all the more suspicious.

For all that, he took me aboard, and I owe him
a profound debt of gratitude. For I am certain
that, had I not broken free from my life in America
when I did, the nervous breakdown from which I
was suffering would have developed into something
more serious and more sinister.

I was given an empty two-berth cabin in an iso-
lated part of the ship's bowels. I think that my
benefactor, the purser, had me put there so that,

should I go mad or run amok, I might not annoy the other passengers.

I stayed on deck till the darkness was settling round the ship, and we were well under way, with clear water ahead. The chill salt air was like a balm to my aching bemused head. Across the gray waters I should find England. I felt calmer and clearer in mind than I had felt for weeks.

With the coming of the dark, I went down to my cheerless little cabin. I felt more tired than I had ever felt in my life, save perhaps on that return-trip from Australia. There was my berth with the white sheet turned down like a great cuff over the coverlet embroidered with the monogram of the Cunard company. I need rack my brain no longer with inventing tragic capers for Churchill's. I could sleep as long as I liked.

Why should I not sleep for the whole length of the voyage? I owed my system a full week's sleep, and here was my chance to make it up. I determined to climb into my berth and not get out of it until we were in the Mersey. I got into the bunk, put my head on the pillow, and immediately slipped down—down—into a deep, kindly well of sleep.

I awoke with a start. Somebody was hammering on the door. A voice called out:

"Aren't you getting up?"

How long had I been asleep, I wondered . . . ? Four days—perhaps even five . . . ? I was certain it had been a long time.

"Aren't you getting up?" the voice repeated. "The second call for dinner has just gone."

"What's the time?" I called back.

"Nearly nine o'clock."

"What night?"

There was a pause, as though of astonishment. Then:

"Sailing-night, of course."

So I had been asleep for less than an hour. I felt viciously that I had been cheated of my right. I got up and opened the door. With an impatient glance at me, the steward entered, carrying a couple of suitcases. There followed him into the apartment another man, a big-framed, broad-shouldered man, but dreadfully thin and pale. He seemed to be in the last stages of weakness, and it seemed to take all his strength to stumble across the floor and flop down on my berth, where he lay panting. His wild-looking eyes, unnaturally bright and enlarged by sickness, stared at me with a kind of intent friendliness.

"This gentleman has come to share this cabin, sir," the steward announced.

I felt like protesting, but did not want to hurt the sick man's feelings. I murmured something about thinking I should be alone, knowing as I did that there were empty cabins all round my own.

The steward gave me a sharp look and said smartly:

"You can complain to the purser, if you like, sir."

Then stowing the newcomer's bags, he left the cabin, snapping the door to behind him.

The man on my berth gasped out:

"Don't like that—feller—much."

"I don't either," I agreed.

We looked at one another, and the sick man smiled. He was dressed and looked like a typical British workman, from his new tweed cap to his thick-soled, well-polished boots. He looked about fifty years of age. Clearly he was seriously ill, and looked all the worse for the fact that it was obviously such a strong body that the disease had eaten up.

He gave me a hasty smile.

"I'll get off your bunk, mate, an' get up on my own—in two secs.—just as soon as I can get my breath."

"Stay where you are," I answered. "I'll take the top berth."

He smiled at me again.

"Mean you're not movin' out o' here?"

"No, I'm staying."

"That's good. Sometimes I get bad turns—an' it's better if there's somebody with you. . . . It's diabetes I've got. . . . They had me in another cabin first, but the other men objected to me bein' with them so they brought me here. . . . It's nice to be settled down."

"What about dinner? It's ready now."

"I shan't go up to the saloon. I'll have it here."

I rang for the steward, and the sick man told him to make the bed and bring him down some dinner. I left to seek out the dining-saloon.

There were few passengers aboard. I sat down in the first vacant seat I saw, which was between two couples who each appeared to be husband and wife. They were decent solid-looking folk with dull faces. The steward brought the *menu* and I ordered my dinner. When I had done so, I saw that the two or three seats on either side of me were vacant. The decent folk to my right and the decent folk on my left had each moved several places away from my contaminating company. Perhaps they had good reason. I must have looked a pretty wild-looking dinner-companion, and had doubtless been glaring about me morosely. For all that, to the discredit of my good sense, I was hurt. I have always preferred those disingenuous people who can be unsociable gracefully to those honest ones who despise to make any bones about it. I thought inimically of the honest folk who had been so admirably frank about refusing to share their cabin with my poor diabetic friend. . . .

The chair next to mine scraped the floor. I glanced round in surprise and saw a man wearing clericals sitting down beside me.

"Good evening," he said pleasantly, then turned to the steward to order his food.

I went on eating moodily. When he had finished ordering, he turned to me again and made some

casual remark about the prospects of the voyage. I
answered him tersely. He went on talking charmingly and easily, and it was not long before I, too,
had thawed. It transpired that he was a Roman
Catholic priest—by name Father Cunningham—a
Glasgow man returning from conducting some mission in America. I am sure now that he must have
seen me being snubbed by my neighbors at the din-
ner-table, and had sat beside me intentionally so
that I should not feel an Ishmael among my fellows.
He was that sort of man; and there was no hint of
patronage in his kindliness. During that voyage,
he was the only soul who spoke a friendly word to
me, with the exception of the poor devil in my cabin.

. . . Not that I was not addressed by the other
passengers. That same night I wandered out on
deck and was staring dully over the side, when a
great slack-jawed man with a Middle-West face and
a Middle-West voice came and tapped me on the
shoulder.

"Pardon me, but I was just wondering down
there if you was a Czech? From your looks, if
you see what I mean—"

"What does it matter to you whether I'm a Czech
or not?" I demanded.

He looked hurt and indignant.

"No harm in asking, is there? Gee, there ain't
no call to bite my nose off just because I asked you
a civil question!"

In the mood of the moment, I was filled with an

overwhelming desire to strike him. I bitterly re-
sented his assumption that he had the right to come
and cross-examine me like this. Little did he know
how near he was to being violently assaulted at that
moment. As it was, I managed to control the sweet
impulse to lay into him. As I walked away without a word, I heard him muttering: "Land's sake!
Some folks sure get het up over nothin'. . . ."

I went below and sought my cabin. The sick man
was undressed and lying in bed. He greeted me
with a friendly nod. I think he had been lonely,
and welcomed my company—such as it was in the
peculiar state of mind I was in.

He nodded to my fiddle-case propped against a
wall.

"What you got there—a fiddle?"

"Yes."

"Can you play it?"

"That's my job."

He looked at me with a kind of nervous eagerness, as if afraid he might be asking too much of me.

"Do us a favor, will you, mate—? Play 'You'll
Remember Me.' "

I took out my fiddle.

"I suppose you mean 'When Other Lips'? It
goes like this. . . ." I played the opening notes, and
he agreed excitedly.

While I played it, he lay back blissfully, his eyes
closed. When I had finished, he smacked his lips
like a chef approving a choice soup.

"Now *that's* music!" he declared. "Real opera, eh? None of your music-hall stuff about that. You know, I think that's the finest song ever written."

I did not tell him that I had rather different views about the song—especially arranged as a violin-solo. He talked avidly for a while, until the talking began to tire him. Then he lay still staring at the bottom of the berth above him. His eyes shone brilliantly. While he talked and after, he drank water incessantly.

I played a little to him quietly, and he went to sleep. I sat watching him for a long time. I knew all his history now. His name was Arthur something. He was a bricklayer and had been living in the States for some time, making money such as he could never have made at the same trade in England. Then he had fallen ill. The doctor had been serious, but had not, I think, told him what the end of the disease must be. Like myself, he had suddenly been seized by an overwhelming instinct to go home. He had said: "Somehow you don't feel so bad when you're at home." His only regret was that he had no relatives to go back to, save some married sister in the Midlands. Poor devil! He was so unconscious of death flying fast behind him. . . . I could have told him that he ought to be glad that he had no relatives.

My pity for him seemed to purge some of the unhealthiness from my own mind. During the period of intense mental strain I had been enduring,

I had been growing more and more introspective. It was good for me now to be feeling for another human-being besides myself. I knew why the steward had brought him to my cabin. I was a queer customer, certainly not fit to mix with the respectable folk aboard, and therefore the only one who might suffer the billeting of a seriously ill man on me. Clearly, they could not put him in a cabin by himself in that condition, and it must have struck them as mighty convenient to have a strange bird such as I aboard to share a roost with this other strange bird. I wonder why they didn't put him straight into the sick-bay? I have a feeling that the cabin-steward had something to do with that. . . .

I went to bed and slept long and late—a giant's feast of sleep. All day I stayed in the cabin with Arthur, leaving him only to go to the saloon at meal-times and eat in company with Father Cunningham. Even the beginning of a normal routine of sleeping and eating and calm thinking was working its cure on me. By the evening my morbidness was almost gone and I could do something I had not done for weeks: I could laugh spontaneously at a joke. My sense of humor was reasserting itself, and that was most important of all: for it meant that my sense of proportion was coming back to me.

Three times that day I played "When Other Lips," to Arthur's great delight. To dilute the dose for my own consumption, I played a number of other things as well. Arthur, with the bogy of pros-

pective loneliness now finally exorcised, was in fine
form, and made little jokes about our "private concerts." He spoke as if they were riots of merry-
making. . . .

The next day I got a shock. I woke after another orgy of sleep and jumped down from my
upper berth to find Arthur sitting up on his and
struggling to pull on a pair of trousers. He waved
to me gaily.

"I'm getting up," he declared. "I feel better
today than I have for weeks."

Not without some qualms, I helped him to dress.

"It's a shame to stay shut up down here," he said.
"I'll get better twice as quickly if I get a sniff or
two of that sea air."

We went slowly up the alleyways and up on deck.
He took great breaths of the air, but began to cough.
He was quiet for a little after that, gazing happily
at the sunshine and the bright water.

"This is grand," he announced. "I feel fit as
that fiddle o' yours below there. Do you know what
I'm going to do? I'm going to go into the smoke-
room and have a bottle of Bass. It's something I've
been lookin' forward to ever since I made up my
mind to take this trip. The stuff you get in the
States ain't the same."

He was like a schoolboy on a stolen holiday. His
eyes were shining at the thought of his own reckless-
ness. To me it seemed that the fever in them was
heightened.

We walked along to the smoke-room. He could only totter in his weakness, but he did not seem to notice it. We sat down at a table and ordered a Bass each. He took a first great gulp of the beer, then finished it in gulps. I think he had a job to drink it all. But he said how much better he felt for the drink.

"This is a celebration," he said. "I'm going to have a cigar now."

He called the wine-steward and asked for "two of the best." He winked at me.

"Come on. We'll smoke these out on deck."

We left the smoke-room and wandered up and down the deck. Arthur, in the full tide of good-fellowship, talked to every second person he passed. Most of them snubbed him (perhaps because of the company he was in!) and all of them passed on quickly. He did not seem to notice their taciturnity. Poor Arthur! He coughed painfully over his cigar, and was staggering about pitifully as we walked. He looked so frail and unsteady on his legs that I was honestly afraid that a strong gust of wind or sudden roll of the boat would knock him over. Before it was nearly half finished, he had to fling his cigar overboard.

We sat down, and Arthur inhaled the breeze exultantly—and coughed. Quite suddenly he said:

"I'm tired. I think I'll go below."

We went back to the cabin. I did not want to endanger his belief in his betterment by offering to help him, but I was tempted to do so several times. When we reached the cabin he was exhausted. I helped him to undress and get into his berth.

"My, it was a treat getting out there," he declared. "What a day it's been!"

He slept for most of the rest of the day, and I began to wonder whether his outing had indeed done him good; but, for all that, I decided before going to bed that night that I should see the ship's surgeon the following morning and get him to see my cabin-mate.

I had barely started undressing when he awoke. "What a day it's been!" he repeated. "Let's finish it off properly. Let's have 'You'll Remember Me'!"

I played it for him very softly. His eyes closed and he seemed to have fallen asleep again. I climbed into my berth. He could not have been asleep, however, for a little later I heard him drinking water.

We had gone to bed early. It must have been still fairly early, when I was aroused by the sound of vomiting. There was a revolting odor in the cabin—something more than the stench of the vomiting. The ugly thought was in my mind that it was like the odor of death itself.

I jumped down out of my bunk, and asked him anxiously if I could do anything for him. He grinned weakly.

"I'm all right. But I've lost that Bass I drank. . . . I thought maybe I wouldn't keep it down."

"I'm going for the doctor," I said.

"No, wait a minute, mate. I'm all right—just bein' sick, that's all. I want company rather than a doctor. . . . Will you do us a favor?"

"Of course. What is it?"

"Play 'You'll Remember Me' just once more. It seems to buck me up, that thing. . . . Oh, I know you've played it already today—but just do it again this once, an' I'll not ask you again."

I put my violin to my chin and played. His face was gaunt and fine-drawn as that of an El Greco saint. His eyes were dark and brilliant. There was a tragic, utterly happy smile on his lips.

His eyes closed. . . .

I stopped playing. His face had taken on a strange greenish pallor which had a livid flush beneath it at the cheek-bones. I bent over him and whispered his name. He did not answer. I took hold of his shoulder and shook him. He made no movement. He was in a coma.

I ran out of the cabin to find the doctor. Flying along the alleyways, I almost ran into Father Cunningham.

"Where are you off to?" he demanded pleasantly.

"To find the doctor. There's a man dying in my cabin."

"What's the number of your cabin?"

I told him and hurried on. When I came back to the cabin with the doctor, we found Father Cunningham inside. He was kneeling by Arthur's berth. Where the light struck it, there was a sheen of oil

on Arthur's brow and on his lips. When Father
Cunningham rose, I saw oil on his finger-tips.

"He is dead," said the priest. "I do not know if
he was a Catholic or not, but I have given him the
Last Sacraments."

The happy smile was still on the dead man's lips.
The doctor leant over the body and covered its face
with the bedsheet. . . .

*　　*　　*

Next day they buried him. After dark, an Angli-
can service was held for some special reason. Most
of the passengers went to the service, and the decks
were almost deserted. I wandered aft to a part of
the boat-deck which was unfrequented at any time
and was now completely solitary. Staring over the
side at the glitter of the black water where it was lit
up from the illuminated deck below, I heard the
drone of voices from that lower deck. A little later
I saw a long box of unpainted wood, rather like a
large packing-case for oranges, being slid out over
the rail below me and dropped over the side. For a
second it floated, then it sank. Later I asked the
doctor about the box, and he told me it was Arthur's
coffin.

When I went back to my cabin that night, I found
the steward there. The dead man's bags were open
òn the floor, and the steward was busy searching for
something under the mattress. When I entered, he
looked rather frightened.

"What are you doing?" I demanded.

He stung himself to defiance.

"*You* know what I'm looking for. Where's his money gone, that's what I want to know? He had some, I know, because he gave me a quid to get some chocolate for him. What have you done with it, eh?"

I felt my stomach rising.

"Get out!" I said.

He changed his front.

"Listen. Split half-and-half with me, and I shan't say a word about it. How about it? You wouldn't like me to go tell the captain all the poor fellow's money's gone, would you?"

I was past speech. I took a step towards him. He must have seen my intention in my eye for he looked scared and backed towards the door.

"I could see you had no time for me the minute you came aboard—" he was beginning, when he stopped short and dived out of the door, closing it just as I leaped at him.

Next day the purser visited me. He was full of apologies for the sick man having been put in beside me, and said I should be placed in another cabin immediately. He said that the steamship company would be glad to refund me my fare for the voyage. I told him that I didn't want my fare back. Let the other ghouls make what they could out of Arthur's death: I would not profit by it.

I was glad to disembark at Liverpool, and I only

saw the *Campania* once again.   It was late in the war, and this "ocean greyhound," once holder of the record for the Atlantic crossing, was lying sunk off the Fife coast in the Firth of Forth, where a German torpedo had struck her.   It was an end not unfitting for my macaber memories of her.

XV

LONDON TANGO

THE threshold of the Great War found me back at the Queen's Theater directing the orchestra. The period was notable for a craze for the tango, and the management of the Queen's saw golden opportunities for profiting by it. They opened the theater on every afternoon when there was no matinee being performed and gave Tango Teas. The Teas were a roaring success, but whether they were the first of these functions which were to become so immensely popular I cannot say.

One of the chief attractions of the tango was that no one could dance it. So that if one could do only one or two steps one could snatch a momentary celebrity. There were of course one or two Argentinos who could go completely through all the complicated movements of the dance—and were duly admired for it—but most people, although they longed to dance like those Argentinos, had no notion of how to go about it.

It was a great chance for the denizens of the hinterland of the Palace Theater. They all had the indispensable swarthiness of accomplished tango dancers, and they all could make a show at some

Latin dance or other. They left their barber's shops and cafés and Mafia circles in Soho and blossomed forth as genuine instructors in the esoteric convolutions of the tango. None of them, of course, knew anything about it, but this one here could do a passable Apache dance, that one there could do the *jota,* and the other could do an obscure Sicilian fandango. As no one knew anything about the tango, no one could deny that these were expert variations of the true South American dance.

The Queen's Tango Teas were crowded, half by moneyed people eager to acquire the fashionable terpsichorean talent of the moment, and half by a strange assortment of dark-skinned Soho waiters, barbers and ladies of the sad sisterhood. The latter half made vast sums of money from the former half as fees for instruction in the tango.

It was a strange and wonderful sight to lead the orchestra and watch the dancers at work. No two couples were unanimous in their steps, and not one was doing the tango. Had I been an Argentino, I should probably have wept in agony. As it was, I was often nearly reduced to tears by the effect on my sense of humor. The instructors and instructresses explained their lack of conformity with the other dancers by the fact that they were performing a localized version of the dance. This uncouth series of movements was a "Peruvian" tango; this was "Bolivian"; this was how they did it among the peaks of the high Andes; that was Chinese, or Moroccan, or Serbian.

Incidentally, among these exponents of the tango, but undoubtedly with a real talent for it, as anyone will agree who saw his interpretation of it in the film "The Four Horsemen of the Apocalypse," was Rudolph Valentino, at that time a waiter in some London hotel.

Although the "professionals," apart from Valentino, were nearly always laughable, there were times when they were annoying. When the excuse about their version of the tango being "Peruvian" did not satisfy the wealthy lady who was paying to be taught the real article, they would blame the orchestra for keeping such bad time that treading upon feminine toes was unavoidable. They would come to me and make indignant complaints.

Eventually I became so weary of such complaints that I told the management that, given the chance, I could give a much better exhibition of the tango than the flat-footed waiters who were plying such a lucrative trade by murdering it. They told me I was welcome to do as I liked about it; so, knowing of a young woman who not only was a brilliant dancer but played the violin as well, I roped her in and evolved a double act in which we played and danced the tango at the same time.

At intervals the rest of the orchestra would have a rest, and my partner and I would do our double-fiddle act. It was very popular, and seemed to impress the Queen's patrons with its genuineness, for after that I had no more complaints about my time and my ignorance of the way to do the dance.

The managers of that theater must have been enterprising people. In the midst of the excitement of the Tango Teas, they staged a mannequin parade. This was a great novelty for pre-war England, and attracted a great deal of attention.

The audience sat in the auditorium of the theater and the mannequins came singly on to the stage. The announcement of the name of the creation would be made—say, "Lisette" or "Jasmine"—and, as the girl entered from the wings, the orchestra would strike up a tune which it played until she took her exit again. For each new creation, we played a new tune.

Next morning the *Daily Mirror* was extraordinarily kind to me. It praised my music handsomely and admired the way in which the spirit of each piece of music fitted each dress which it heralded. It declared that I must have studied the colors of the dresses and made a most "particular choice of music to suit each color."

I am glad that the music was so suitable. The fact is, however, that during the parade I had a pile of music beside me and hurriedly grabbed the first piece that came to my hand. Not for the first time, my faith in the critical qualities of the press was imperiled.

* * *

Early in the war, I was engaged to play privately for both Sir Alfred and Robert Mond on a succession of occasions, and came to see a great deal of

them.   On one occasion a New Year tableau was
given at a house party, and I was cast for the part of
Father Time.   I was a signal failure.   I was supposed to come on, with beard, scythe and hour-glass,
half-draped, and say a few seasonably witty words.
But when it comes to speaking—public or otherwise
—I do not shine.   What was worse, I developed, for
the first time in my life, a bad attack of stage fright.
Feeling horribly self-conscious, I shambled on in
my strange get-up, mumbled half-a-dozen completely unintelligible words, and shambled hurriedly
off again.   I knew that the producer of the tableaux
would be after my blood, and also after me to try
and persuade me to go through the nerve-shattering
experience of showing myself on the platform again.
So I disappeared, and did not show up again until
the tableaux were over.

I was very friendly with Sir Alfred's secretary,
and one day was told by him that Sir Alfred, as a
mark of appreciation for the playing I had done for
him, was going to present me with a certain diamond
scarf-pin which I had openly admired.   Sir Alfred,
my friend the secretary said, was bringing the pin
down from his London house the following day, and
would hand the pin to the secretary to give to me.

Next day I went to see the latter to collect my
gift.   Imagine the shock I received when I was
greeted with the news that he was dead. . . . He
had had a stroke and died within an hour or so.

Later it appeared that, by a curious turn of fate,

he had been wearing the scarf-pin which he was going to give me from Sir Alfred Mond. The pin was accepted as being his own property, and of course I was much too disturbed by his sudden death to claim it as mine.

Sir Alfred Mond, however, found out in some way that I had never received his gift, so he gave me another. This was a fine black Welsh pony that I had ridden several times while staying with Sir Alfred.

I was delighted with my present, and, as I was wandering the roads with my caravan at the time, took the pony with me. We came to Westerham for the Horse Show, and I exhibited the pony in the Tradesmen's Class of entries. It won the second prize. Very pleased with myself, I betook myself to that part of the fair-ground where a concert was being held at which I was engaged to play solos. There I met my accompanist, a dark, notably handsome young man. We shook hands. I told him my name and asked his.

"Ivor Novello," he said.

I had not heard the name before.

"What are you going to play?" he asked.

I brought out a wad of music, and we looked through it together. One after another piece he pulled out in disgust and flung down.

"Popular stuff!" he said contemptuously.

He selected a Brahms concerto and the "Prize Song" from the *Mastersingers*.

"These seem to be about the best you've got," he said. "Shall we play these for a start?"

"Yes, if you think they'll go down here."

"That doesn't matter. As artists, it's our duty to ourselves to play music worthy of ourselves. If the public wants popular stuff, it'll just have to be disappointed."

We played. Partly out of high spirits, partly to get a little of my own back, I played little tricks with the Brahms concerto. I put in trills and grace-notes and eccentric incidentals and bird-calls. The pianist glared at me, but the audience liked it.

In the middle of the applause, I saw a lady striding towards us. I had not heard of Ivor Novello in those days, but I recognized this lady immediately as a famous figure in the singing world. It was Clara Novello-Davies.

"That," she said to me, "was murder."

"Madame Novello-Davies," I answered, "it was."

"Then why did you do it?"

I nodded towards Ivor.

"To annoy the pianist here. He tore up all my popular music."

"What a pity! I'm sure it just suited your style of playing."

It was time to start our encore. I put even more bird's chirps, etc., into the "Prize Song" than I had into the concerto; but later, when we played some Correlli Variations, I played the music as written.

"That's better," said Ivor.

"I hope it'll please my other critic," I retorted.

"I'm sure it will. Mother is no fonder of vulgar-
izing good music than I am."

So this was Clara Novello-Davies's son! I looked
at him suspiciously, and he was smiling. I began to
laugh. . . . Presently Madame Novello-Davies herself came across to me again and was most charming.
After a somewhat unpromising beginning, we parted
on the best of terms.

It must have been very shortly afterwards that the
highbrow young pianist wrote that terrific popular
success, "Keep the Home Fires Burning."

At the very next fair-ground that I moved to after
leaving Westerham, I ran into disaster.

I had been working at this fair-ground for some
days, plying a good trade as a horse doctor in the
Petulengro tradition. Among other jobs I had done
was one of scoring the teeth of a certain horse as a
cure for the disease of *lampus*. A couple of days
after doing the job, I was told that a policeman had
come to the fair-ground looking for me. I sought
him out and asked him what he wanted with me.

"I want to take you in charge. There's a charge
against you of bishoping a horse's teeth."

"But that's not true!" I protested.

"Maybe not, but there's witnesses who say you
have been bishoping. You'll have to come along
with me."

And, as he said, I had to go along with him.
Bishoping, be it noted, is a practise well known to

gypsies of the Petulengro class, as it is also to most dishonest horse dealers. As everybody knows, a horse's age can be told roughly by examining its teeth—unless an expert bishoper has been at work; for a bishoper can, with a red-hot iron, sculpture the teeth of an aged hack into the authentic shape of a colt's. It is, of course, a thief's practise, but it has also been suggested by certain humane societies that it is cruel to the horse. This, personally, I doubt, for I am sure that scoring for *lampus,* which is a somewhat similar operation to that of bishoping, does not give the horse any real pain, though he will probably shy at the approach of the red-hot iron.

I knew immediately, of course, that, unless this charge of bishoping had been deliberately trumped-up against me by some enemy, some person, probably in all sincerity, had seen me doing the scoring for *lampus* and had thought I was bishoping.

I was brought up before a large plum-faced magistrate who looked just like one of Mr. H. M. Bateman's generals. The charge was read, and the color of his face deepened alarmingly. He was in the last throes of indignation. I felt exactly as, I am sure, the Guardsman felt when he dropped his rifle on parade! Later I found out that he rode regularly with the local pack of hounds, and that he was a great lover of horses.

Unfortunately for me, however, he knew very little about horses. I explained to him about having performed the operation for *lampus,* but he had never heard of it. But he *had* heard of bishoping. I was not the first gypsy to be brought before him on that charge. He simply would not listen to a word I had to say. He had seen my kind before. We were rogues and horse-torturers to a man. My excuse about the *lampus* operation was childish. Of course I had been bishoping; and that was much more than an illegal action. It was a crime against God and the name of humanity—it was the unforgivable crime—it was cruelty to a horse. The fine he imposed on me was a savage one.

I wonder if I should have got off more lightly if I had worn hunting pink instead of moleskins at the court?

XVI

A DRINK WITH MICHAEL COLLINS

THE War Book, that very specialized branch of literature, has been invented to deal particularly with all events taking place between the years 1914-18. So, this not being a War Book, I shall cheerfully mutilate this autobiography by carving out of it all that befell me during that period.

. . . Somewhere about 1919-20, I was traveling across the face of Ireland by night, bound from Dublin to Cork. In these days of the Rebellion, Dublin had some ugly sights to show. I had seen men shot out of hand in doorways, in the open street, even in tramcars. I had seen one shot in the alley at the back of the theater in which I had been performing in a vaudeville act.

I was glad to be out of Dublin, little knowing that the "Troubles" there were being duplicated in Cork —only they were twice as bad. As the train rumbled south, I believed I was leaving the storm center. In reality, I was hastening towards it.

I began to realize that even before we reached Cork. We were just coming into Mallow, when the train stopped with a jerk that almost flung me on to the seat opposite. I put my head out of the window, but the night was very dark, and I could see nothing.

Along the length of the train, doors were opening and people were demanding to know the cause of the stoppage. Some of them were jumping out and going towards the front of the train. I opened the door of my own compartment and jumped out, and walked in the direction of the engine. Standing about it were a small body of the Royal Irish Constabulary and a few Auxiliaries. Among the passengers also standing about, a great deal of excited talk was going on.

"What's the matter?" I asked an elderly man near me.

"It's Mallow Bridge. It's been blown up. Lucky for us we weren't crossing at the time."

"We can't see what's left of the bridge from here, can we?"

"I don't know. I'm a stranger here. You might."

I moved outward from the track to see ahead, the stranger coming with me. Against the dark sky ahead I saw the loom of some irregularly shaped object. I pointed to it.

"That isn't it, is—?"

I had no time to finish the sentence. There was the crack of a gun, and a bullet sang close past my head, and went whining away into the darkness.

Instinctively, I flung myself flat on the ground. The group of R.I.C. men at the head of the train came running toward me. One of them hauled me to my feet and dug the muzzle of a revolver against my stomach.

"Where's that gun? I saw ye. Come on, hand it over, or—!"

"Got a gun, has he?" demanded a man in the uniform of a sergeant, and began searching me.

"If he had one, he's dropped it. See if ye can find it on the ground about here, boys," he said after satisfying himself that I was unarmed.

"Wait a minute!" I interrupted indignantly. "This fellow here had a shot at me for no reason at all—and nearly hit me, too. I haven't got a gun, and I never have a gun."

"Oh, yes, ye had," retorted the man who was holding his revolver to my stomach. "I saw his arm against the sky. Pointing it this way, he was."

"It was my finger I was pointing. I saw something ahead that I thought was the broken bridge, and I was pointing to it. Then you let fly at me."

It was a long time before I could convince them that I was telling the truth. Even the elderly man I had been talking to was for a while under suspicion of being my accomplice in attempted assassination. The face of the man who had fired the shot at me was strained and haggard. His nerves must have been taut as bowstrings with the strain he and the other members of the R.I.C. had been undergoing for months past. At last I convinced them of my pacific intentions.

The sergeant said bruskly:

"All right, I believe ye. But take my advice. Don't be pointing at anything ye see in Ireland these days!"

I went back to my compartment—and stayed there. Not for long, however. After a while we were shepherded out of the train and across country to Mallow, where we crossed the Blackwater by the footbridge.

On the other side of the river we waited for another train to take us to Cork. It was the early hours of the morning before it arrived. During that wait, I thought, for the second time that night, that my last minute had arrived. A soldier, wearing the Tam-o'-Shanter of the Black-and-Tans came blundering among the waiting passengers. He was drunk, and from his right hand he was swinging a revolver by its lanyard.

He was in an ugly mood, and he glared from one to another of us as if inviting us to speak so that he might put us in our places for it. He twirled the revolver on its string recklessly. There was a very real danger of its going off and killing somebody.

Among us was a pretty girl. He went up to her and fondled her cheek. As she drew away, he frowned angrily and made to grab her round the waist. She smacked his face. He stood glaring at her, pouring out a flood of filthy words at her, then he jumped forward to grab her again.

I took a step forward. Hearing the movement behind him, he checked himself and turned to face me. For several seconds we stood quite still staring at one another fixedly. The madness of a beast was in his eyes. He began to swing his revolver again. He caught it by the butt and moved towards me.

"This is the end," I thought. "Whether I stand here or jump at him, he'll shoot me. I haven't a chance."

. . . A voice called out a name. A second man in the uniform of the Black-and-Tans with two more behind him was standing behind the first. By his Sam Browne belt, he appeared to be an officer. He walked slowly up to the first man, then with ferocious suddenness grabbed his revolver and wrenched it completely off its lanyard. The force of the tug sent the drunken man staggering forward. The officer snapped out an order to the two men at his back. They advanced with rifles leveled, and, at a nod from the officer, marched the first man off. . . .

*   *   *

I wandered into the bar of the Palace Court Theater in Cork. The performance was just starting in the auditorium, and I was due to begin my turn in about an hour.

Standing at one end of the counter was a group of seven or eight men. As I entered, I glanced at them. One I recognized immediately. He was a notorious rebel called Larry O'Lynch. A second later I recognized a second member of the group. It was Michael Collins himself. I knew him at once for I had

already been introduced to him by my good friend
Mike Nono at a party in Merrion Square, Dublin.
There he stood as large as life. There was a large
price on his head, and a complete indifference in
his demeanor. He leaned against the bar in the
brightly-lit public place with as much ease as if he
were safe from peril in some mountain cabin. Had
the representatives in Ireland of the British Government known he was in the theater—in Cork even—
they would have gone almost hysterical with excitement.

He smiled recognition at me and I walked across
to his side. I was talking to him about some mutual
friends, when Dick McGrath, the manager of the
theater, entered the bar and came straight across to
my side.

"There's a man here looking for you," he said,
and handed me a card.

I looked at it. It bore the name of Captain Holbrook.

"He says he knows you."

"I don't know him."

"Then he's not coming in here," said Dick. He
nodded towards Collins's men and whispered: "Not
with these boys here. It's the 'Captain' in his name
I don't like."

"Wait a minute, though," I said. "There's a Captain Holbrook who used to be friendly with one of
my brothers. He may be taking me for my brother."

Dick was silent for a moment, then said dubiously:

"Well, if he's a friend of your brother's, I suppose it's all right. I'll tell him you're here."

I turned to resume my conversation with Collins.

"There's a friend of my brother's coming here to look for me," I said.

A few minutes later Dick McGrath entered with three other men. I heard one word whispered by the group beside me: *"Tans. . . ."*

They stared across the room at the three strangers. Their faces were hard and set, and the right hand of each man was in his jacket pocket. It seemed that next moment I should see the three newcomers killed before my eyes.

As to the three, there was none of them whom I recognized as the Holbrook of my brother's acquaintance. Equally, none of them gave any sign of recognizing me. They moved to the opposite end of the bar and called for drinks. McGrath came across to our group.

"There's some mistake," I whispered to him urgently. "This isn't the Holbrook I know."

"Then who the hell are these fellows!"

"They're Tans, Dicky," said Collins quietly.

"Listen, Mike," McGrath implored him. "Don't start shooting here. Once you start, it'll mean reprisals, and it'll be the end of this theater."

Collins had not heard my whisper to McGrath about not knowing the strangers. He glanced round at his men and nodded towards me.

"Keep your guns in your pockets, boys," he ordered. "These fellows are friends of his."

"They're Tans, Mike."

"I know, but you'll have to make it some other time."

Meanwhile the three men at the other end of the bar must have recognized the leader of my group. They stood there silent, unmoving, their drinks waiting untouched on the bar. There was a horrible dumb fear written on their faces. Later I discovered that they had heard a rumor that Michael Collins was in the theater, and had come in mufti to test the rumor, believing him to be alone. They had seen my name on the playbills outside and had used it simply in order to go where they liked about the building. It must have been a nasty shock to find the rebel leader with half-a-dozen of his men.

At a nod from Collins, his men began to walk slowly across the floor towards the door. To do so, they had to pass the other group. The latter must have thought their last hour had come, and their relief must have been painful when Collins and his men walked straight past them and out of the bar.

By not shooting these three men out of hand, Collins was taking an almost suicidal risk. Well-known as he was in Cork, every Government sympathizer was on the alert to look for him. Yet there he was wandering publicly in the town. To add to that the fact that three of the Auxiliaries had recognized him and had been allowed to remain free to

raise the hue-and-cry was almost madness. Yet
Collins was the kind of man who did things like
that, and I believe it was his brazen taking of fool-
hardy risks that kept him safe for so long.

As it was, Holbrook and his two companions
waited only long enough to let Collins's men get out
of the building, then they rushed out of the bar.
Within a few minutes, the hunt would be up for
Collins all over Cork. . . .

McGrath relaxed limply against the bar and let
out his breath in a great sigh.

"Two John Jamiesons—doubles," he said weakly
to the bartender.

We drank them neat. We needed them. It had
not been pleasant standing between two bodies of
armed men, just in the line of fire.

"Our troubles aren't over for the night," he announced fretfully. "There's a crowd of the bright
boys downstairs, and God knows what'll happen
when we play 'God Save the King.' "

"Then why play it?"

"We've got to play it. If we don't, the Black-and-
Tans'll wreck the place."

"That's hard. Who's the poor devil who's going
to play it?"

"You are," he said simply.

Frankly, the prospect did not appeal to me. I
told him so. But he assured me that no danger attached to the mere player of the tune: besides it was
unlikely that the rebel sympathizers would dare to

express themselves openly in Cork, with martial law in force and soldiers everywhere. In the end, he persuaded me, and anyone who knew Dicky Mc-Grath will know that he had a genius for persuading people to do things against their will and better judgment.

I gave my own performance about the middle of the bill. The show went on and presently the curtain fell on the last turn. Now came my ordeal, and McGrath was at my elbow to see that I did not refuse the fence at the last moment.

The curtain parted again. I came out in front and began to play. I got about as far as the sixth bar, with a third of the audience on their feet and the rest sitting down—and then the riot started. There was a wild yell of indignation, then a solitary shot—then a fusillade. I took one dive off the stage into the orchestra-well and another down the con-ductor's bolt-hole. Momentarily safe under the stage, I listened to the pandemonium in the audi-torium. The crackle of shots went on, intermingled with the unmistakable sounds of a first-class panic. The shooting fell off for a while as the people fought to get out of the exits. It was providential that the exits were open, and that the audience had been a small one.

For a time there was no sound but the uproar of the people battling their way out of the theater, and there were no more shots. Then, when most of them must have got out, there came muffled from outside the building the vicious yammering of machine-gun fire.

For several minutes rifle and machine-gun fire went on sporadically, then the climax of that eventful evening came. There was a terrific explosion that rocked the whole building on its foundations.

It was not till several hours later, when the firing had ceased and Cork, for the moment, was a city of calm, that we ventured out of our hiding-places to see what had been happening outside. The explosion had done its work thoroughly. The whole front of the theater had been blown up and hung in a crazy wreck on its shattered pillars. Poor Dicky McGrath!

XVII

THE ROAD TO AFRICA

THE world whirls through time into a new distinctive period. The trailing clouds that the war has left behind have been forcibly swept away. Cheated since 1914 of its lightheartedness, the world leaps madly to make up what it has lost in a flying career of hectic living. It is the feverish 1920's.

By now I am appearing regularly in a vaudeville act with my gypsy girl partner, Maachah, and two performing dogs, Foxy and Danny. We are offered an engagement in Africa, and sail for Cape Town. With us travel Sable Fern, Leo Dryden, Lily Burnand and Charlie Lee, veterans of the variety stage who are going out to give one of the first of these "old stagers" shows, the revivals of which are to become so popular.

At Cape Town we participate in a civic welcome given to our more elderly fellow-artists. By the time we assemble in the theater to give our show, the veterans are in hilarious mood. The hospitality has been lavish, and they are like old race-horses, long kept in the stables, who suddenly and unexpectedly find themselves in the open again, with the turf stretching away in front of them once more.

Interest in the reappearance of these old favorites has been immense in the city. The hall is packed, and the deputy-mayor is there to introduce every performer as he or she comes on.

Sable Fern is first. The deputy-mayor precedes her, and tells the audience that they need no introduction to this artiste. They all remember with what pleasure they heard her, in the days gone by, singing the song she made her own: "What's the Use of Loving a Girl?" And there and then, he proceeds to sing through the entire song. It is quite a triumph for him that he is word-perfect, but poor Sable Fern's style is somewhat cramped when she has to sing a song that somebody else has just gone completely through.

Leo Dryden is next. The deputy-mayor reminds them of how feelingly Leo used to render his great number, "The Miner's Dream of Home." Would they like a sample of it? And therewith, he gives them the whole song as a sample. When Leo sings, the audience applaud him to the echo, but clearly the first, fine careless rapture has been rubbed off his singing.

The deputy-mayor announces the next artiste— Lily Burnand. It seems but yesterday since first they heard her singing so charmingly "Two Little Girls in Blue." Do they remember it? How could they forget? At least he has not forgotten; and, to prove it, he lets them hear it. Once again, he is word-perfect.

While Lily Burnand is giving the second rendering of her song, Charlie Lee, Cockney comedian, is standing in the wings making strange noises under his breath. He is due to go on next, and is eying the deputy-mayor in no amiable fashion. Charlie has not been unappreciative of the typical South African hospitality that has preceded the performance. . . .

Lily finishes her song and comes off to deafening applause. The deputy-mayor advances to announce the next item.

He is given no chance. He opens his mouth to speak, but, before he can get a word out, Charlie rushes on to the stage and pushes him aside. The audience cheer him to the echo.

"That's right!" Charlie shouts back. "You know me all right—Charlie Lee. Now we'll get on with the show!"

And, after that, they do!

*   *   *

Our African tour ends at Durban, and Maachah and I, responding to the call of the wild, hire horses and tents, and, with Foxy and Danny, ride northward.

We leave the railhead behind at Kranskop, and cross the Tugela into Zululand. The first day of our ride across the river, numbers of natives cross our path going in the same direction. A tribal dance is being held somewhere, and they are massing for it.

As darkness comes down, we see more and more Zulus trekking. Evidently we are near the place where the dance is to take place. I suggest stopping to pitch our camp, but Maachah is nervous and is against lighting a fire. We decide to ride on for a while longer. It is moonlight now, and still there are shadowy figures moving across the plain.

We pull up sharply. Straight ahead of us a wagon makes a black pattern against the sky. We approach it. It is empty and derelict. Maachah whispers to me: "Let's climb up into the driving-seat and stay there till daylight. I couldn't sleep in my tent to-night."

We climb up to the rickety buckboard and hunch ourselves on the driving-seat. The dogs are nervous and huddle against us, where they lie unmoving. As we sit there, we still see an occasional dark figure flitting past in the moonlight. It is inexpressibly weird. Fearful for the safety of the horses, I tie their reins to my wrist.

Suddenly the moon goes out. The night is as pitch-black as the inside of a tomb. There is dead silence save for the sound of the wind in the grass, yet I know that figures are still passing in the darkness. We sit there alert, unspeaking, listening intensely—for what? The dogs are shivering. The horses are moving restlessly.

With frightening abruptness, the dogs begin to

bark viciously. Instinctively I tug at the reins round my wrist. At the end of one pair I feel the resistance of the horse's mouth, but the other pair has been cut through no more than a foot from my wrist. Even as I realize this, I hear the other horse go stampeding away into the blackness.

In a moment I have jumped down from the wagon seat to the ground. But the blackness is so thick that I can see nothing farther than a yard from my eyes. There is no sign of the horse, nor of the man who has cut its rein. I cannot understand how, even though he must have crept up so silently that I could not hear him, the horses and the dogs did not sense his presence before they did.

"What's wrong?" Maachah calls out. Everything had happened so quickly that she knows nothing save that the dogs have barked and I have jumped down from the wagon.

"One of the horses has gone. Someone's cut the rein from my wrist."

She jumped down beside me.

"I don't like this. Let's take the horse we've got left and turn back towards the river."

There is an eeriness in the thick dark, peopled with silent figures in our imagination—in the silence, in the theft of the horse—that touches both of us with intangible fear.

"Yes," I say. "Let's turn back."

We pack our tents on the remaining horse and turn back towards the Tugela on foot. It is daylight before we reach the river. We cross over, and leave Zululand—without regrets.

*   *   *

We are in the midst of deck-sports on the voyage home. The great personage aboard is Admiral Sir —— returning from his command of the China Station. He is umpire when I defeat his Flag-Lieutenant in that boisterous game in which two men try to knock one another off a greasy pole with bolsters. It is the final tie of the tournament, so I am greasy-pole champion of the ship!

The victory is not popular with some of the young naval officers traveling with the Admiral. I wear long hair and earrings, and am not fond of drinking at the bar and listening to naughty stories, and it jars on their sense of fitness that such an effeminate creature has laid their champion low.

The Admiral announces my victory, and the second-class passengers cheer loudly, for I am one of them. Then the Admiral challenges me to a cock-fight, and the young officers, who have reserved their applause, let themselves go.

The circle is drawn on the deck, and the Admiral and myself are trussed up so that we can only hop with our legs bent up under us. The loser is the combatant who is pushed out of the circle most often by his opponent. I mean the Admiral to play that part; but, although my senior in years, he is still very nimble as well as strong. I win the first fall, and he the next. In the third and final round, he gets me on my back and is slowly but surely edging me over the chalk line, when I call my acrobatic training to my aid. I do an "upstart" (that is, I jump in one movement from my back on to my feet), recover the advantage, and, before the Admiral can position himself properly, knock him out of the ring.

I am promptly challenged by another officer to a second bout of cock-fighting, but the second-class passengers protest loudly that I cannot fight again immediately after my battle with the Admiral. The match is postponed until the following day.

Meanwhile there is a pot of surprising bitterness brewing between the first- and second-class passengers. The former maintain that my use of the "upstart" maneuver was cheating, and the latter deny it hotly. Ridiculously large sums of money are being betted on my coming encounter with the officer; and a number of hearty members of my second-class supporters announce that they are going to put me into training for the fray. Their idea of training seems to consist chiefly of pouring large quantities of Guinness down my throat at the bar of the second-class smoke-room.

. . . It is the day of the great encounter. Practically every passenger aboard is there to watch. There is more bitter argument and more betting. The combat starts, and I win the first fall. My opponent is not in the same class as the Admiral as a

cock-fighter; he gets me on my back, but, to a howl
of execration from the enemy supporters, I regain
my feet by use of the contentious "upstart."

I begin hustling him across to the chalk line.
Some of the first-class passengers surreptitiously
keep him from being shoved over it by pushing him
back with their feet. I begin to get annoyed. I
make a reckless charge at him which sends him
crashing right through the ring of spectators and
into the scuppers. There is bilge-water in the scuppers, and he is ill-pleased. He mutters something
dark about not being content until our athletic ri-
valry is settled in the gym, with boxing-gloves. But
the Admiral persuades us to shake hands. We dislike one another, but we agree to do so for the sake
of form.

Meanwhile the second-class passengers are shouting their heads off with triumphant joy. They had
all won their bets. There'll be a hot time in the
smoke-room tonight. . . .

*   *   *

I am playing in Falkirk, and the audience seems
extraordinarily enthusiastic. Every second note I
play is greeted by clapping—or a sound very like it.
I am a little deaf, but the applause seems very loud
to me. At the same time I am conscious of the theater being uncomfortably hot.

Then I see a strange thing. In the midst of this
terrific applause (or what sounds very like it),
people, staring at me with looks of horror, are get-

ting up from their seats and hurrying from the theater. I finish my number and bow, but by this time, despite the clapping-sound that is still going on, the theater is half empty. I turn to go off, and discover the cause of the mystery. The backcloth is a mass of flames!

The manager comes out in front and tells the audience's backs that the fire is a small one confined to the stage and well under control already, and that there is no cause for alarm. Then the fire-curtain comes down.

The manager comes up to me and shakes my hand fervently.

"Well done, old boy!" he declares. "You've done marvelously. God knows how many lives you've saved, playing there with the fire roaring behind you."

I do not explain that, owing to my deafness, I have mistaken the crackling of the flames for the applause of the audience.

Some time later I am presented with a medal from some society as a reward for my coolness in the face of great danger in going on playing while the stage was burning about me and thus averting a dangerous panic. Such is the making of a hero. On one occasion, at any rate, my playing did not lack warmth.

*   *   *

Our liner is just about to leave the lovely harbor of Colombo, in which town I have just ended an engagement. Another man and myself are swimming round the vessel, and the passengers high over our heads are leaning over the rail watching us.

A woman screams shrilly. Voices shout down to us in panic. I make out the word "shark."

By good luck I am not far from a bos'un's ladder. Cutting the water, I see two triangular fins. They are coming toward us from the direction of the open sea at a terrifying pace. I waste no time, but make for the ladder at top-speed. My companion has a little farther to swim in order to reach it, but he is a famous swimmer and I think he will reach the side in time.

But I underestimate the speed of the sharks' approach. I am about a yard from the ladder to safety, when I hear a dreadful human scream, quickly stifled, from behind me, and a nauseating crunching sound. One of the sharks has caught his prey.

My hand touches the ladder. I scramble up it in such haste that I catch my right knee a heavy blow on the side. I have barely climbed to the second rung, when I hear the swish and swirl of the great fish's turn in the water less than two feet below me.

My knee is so painful that it is all I can do to climb to the deck. When I reach it, I collapse and cannot get up again. I have to be supported to my cabin. Later I am found to have smashed my knee-cap.

I am soon hobbling about again, but the horrible death of my fellow-swimmer has cast a gloom over me which lasts till the end of the voyage. I have been at my animal-collecting again in Ceylon, and am bringing a large consignment home with me. My geckos and chameleons are roosting all over the rigging, and there are stranger creatures still in my cabin. I have to bribe a seaman to go aloft and bring my pets down from the rigging when their mealtimes come round. I have also great difficulty in providing them with their customary *menus*. Flies are at a premium for dietary purposes, and most of the crew have been enrolled as fly-catchers.

There is a couple aboard who intrigue me: a mother and daughter. The daughter is notably good-looking, and the mother is a typical flighty innocuous Anglo-Indian—at least she appears to be innocuous.

They are professional card-sharpers. A few nights ago they lifted a large sum from two wealthy Jewish brothers. The mother stacks the cards, and the daughter is the foil. The technique of the latter is to fall apparently madly in love with some man or other, who with his vanity titillated by the obvious devotion of this beautiful creature is easily persuaded by the creature's mother to take a hand in a "little game." The daughter, be it noted, is bored with cards, evidently, and doesn't play at all well— evidently. . . . She affects impatience with "mother's awful passion for these horrid games." When the *watler* has lost all the money he is likely to lose, the girl transfers her infatuation to some other male object—not sharply and brutally, but with a delicacy which is completely convincing.

In order to test the knowledge of card-sharping taught me by the great Gunthie in Australia these many years before, I sit in with the mother at a few games of *vingt-et-un* and poker. She must be a much cleverer sharper than even Gunthie, however, for I cannot once detect how she has stacked the cards. The strange thing is that, although I have never played with her save for the very lowest stakes, she is always eager to play with me and lift my few shillings, when there are no bigger fish to be caught. I honestly believe that she loves cheating for the sake of cheating itself. She teaches me that, even in crime, one need not be entirely mercenary.

*   *   *

I am out with the Essex Union. I am wearing pink, riding a good-looking mount, and I have paid my hunt fee. Such being so, nobody pays a great deal of attention to me, although my seat in the saddle is an inelegant crouch that was never taught in a riding-school. I wonder how my fellow huntsmen and huntswomen would react if I were to inform them that I hoped the run would not be too long as I was due to appear in an acrobatic dancing act at the first house of the Holborn Empire?

Or if I were to remind them of my early hunts—not as legitimate follower of the Delaware, or the Essex Union, or the Somerset Staghounds, as in my

present period—but as an unwelcome and unorna-
mental trailer behind any pack of hounds that I
happened to see meeting? In those days gone by,
I should not have been in pink and a topper, but in
dirty ratcatcher and hatless, my long hair flying in
the wind and my earrings glittering. I should have
paid no fees, but simply followed when hounds
began to run. I should have been mounted on a
bareback Welsh cob.

Yet for all that I should have taken my fences
straighter than most of them, and kept up with the
leaders as well as today on my well-saddled good-
looking chestnut. What is more, my wild past self
would have enjoyed the run every bit as well as my
present respectable self.

. . . The run is not too long after all. We kill
after an hour, and I am able to get back to London
in ample time for my appearance at the Holborn
Empire.

It is a tragic appearance for me. I am "cobbling"
during a Russian dance, when I feel a stab of pain
in the knee-cap I injured while escaping from the
shark in Colombo Harbor, and my right leg col-
lapses under me. I am an old enough hand at the
game to hide the fact that anything has gone wrong,
however, and my partner covers me up well. I do
not think the audience notices anything, and that is
what counts, after all. . . . But I am finished for
acrobatic dancing. Lucky for me that dancing is
not my sole means of livelihood. . . .

XVIII

PICKING UP DIAMONDS

THE 1920's have almost run themselves out, and I am once more in Africa with my three good partners, Maachah, Foxy and Danny. We came out on a contract with the African Trust, but considered that they had made arrangements for a tour which was not the tour set down on the contract. In consequence, instead of appearing in the Trust's circuit of halls, we have instigated a law-suit against them and resigned ourselves to work outside the theater for the meantime.

Both Maachah and myself are attracted to the idea of diamond-mining, particularly as we have met, through a friend, a Boer prospector who has found stones worth thousands of pounds. This prospector, Raau, has told us that he has found a place near Razemabrook where there is blue clay and—he believes—diamonds. We agree to grub-stake him, and prepare to become diamond-diggers.

First I apply to a friend of mine who is a Justice of the Peace, and, two licensed diggers having vouched for me, I am presented with my prospector's license at Clarksdorp for the sum of one shilling. The convenient J.P. also procures me four

black boys as laborers from a Labor Camp. I un-
dertake to pay them at the rate of £1 a month, with
mealie-pap and a blanket each thrown in. Raau has
attended to the buying of the digging implements
we shall need, and now we are ready to fare forth
to our future Rand.

We go by donkey-train to Razemabrook, and from
there we trek forty miles to the vicinity of the Waal
River. At the prompting of Raau, we pitch our
camp.

This Raau is a curious customer, and I find it
difficult to open my heart to him. He is a cousin of a
Boer leader, and like most of them has at one time
been engaged in the horse trade. He has a rooted
objection to roughing it, and insists before the trip
starts on importing from Johannesburg the latest
thing in tents, an officer's camp-bed and a bulky
easy-chair—all for his own use and comfort.

We stake out our claim—the regulation thirty feet
by thirty—and begin digging. The black boys will
not work beyond a certain pace, but they will work
at that pace all day, and I am content with them.
Raau, on the other hand, is disgusted. Even though
he must know that nothing will make them work any
faster, he has the Boer's ineradicable conviction that
a nigger works better and is happier if he is being
larded at frequent intervals with a *sjambok*. So he
keeps his whip in his hand all day, and drives the
boys unceasingly. He tells me triumphantly that
I don't know how to handle niggers, but I notice

that, although they may spurt in their digging for a second or two after receiving the lash, they make up for it afterwards by slacking. Also, I doubt if trying to make them work any faster is economically wise. Water has to be brought all the way from the Waal by a man who makes water-carrying his profession—and probably it is a lucrative profession, too, for I have to pay half-a-crown for each kerosene-tin of water he brings. The result is that when the boys are being driven too hard and are sweating a great deal they drink water incessantly, making the provision of water one of the heaviest running expenses of the camp.

Now we have reached the blue clay, and Raau is driving the natives harder than ever. The bill for water is alarming. Some half of our thirty feet square have been dug, and Maachah goes down into the hole and idly examines the clay. Suddenly she gives a yell:

"I've found one! I've found a diamond!"

Raau and I come rushing out of our tents, doubting that she has found anything of the sort, but half-believing that it is a diamond she has found. She is holding a dirty-gray stone in her hand. Without a word, Raau snatches it from her, scrapes it with his knife, and peers at it. We watch his face in breathless excitement.

"It is a diamond," he grunts. "A good one, too."

It has happened—we have discovered a new mine! That night I give the boys extra tit-bits with their rations. The next day I literally ply them with water.

That night Raau comes to my tent.

"That diamond the lady found. I'll give you £25 for it."

"How much is it worth?" I ask.

He is silent for a second, then he says:

"Perhaps £100—but you must know a licensed buyer. I have my own ways of selling it. That's why you must sell it to me for so much less than it's worth."

I shake my head obstinately. I have no great liking for Raau, and I think his offer is miserly, despite his frankness in admitting he is underbidding for the stone.

"I'll keep the diamond."

"You won't get as much as £15 from a licensed buyer."

"Even so, I still prefer to keep it."

"You are being foolish, but you know your own business best."

He gets up sullenly and leaves the tent.

In the next week or two we discover several more stones, all smaller than Maachah's first find. As obliged by law, we duly report our discovery, and presently the Government decides to proclaim our mine as a new diamond-field. I know what this will mean. On a certain day, the field will be declared open, and the prospectors will line up and, at the word "go," race across country to stake out their claims. Under such an arrangement, Raau and I will be allowed to share thirty claims between us as discoverers.

The day comes when the new field is declared open. In the afternoon we see the first of the claim-stakers. They come running towards our camp and stake out their regulation patches of thirty feet by thirty all round us. Most of them are "greasy-axles" of the inveterate miner type. It is not long before they are calling on us to demand, in the name of African hospitality, the food they have not them-selves. In the name of the same sacred code, we do not hesitate, but give them what they want immedi-ately.

Meanwhile the mine is not paying as well as our first find seemed to promise. We are getting few stones out, and they are all small. This, looked on in conjunction with the amount of food and water I have handed out to the needy newcomers, makes me wonder how long my pocket will be able to stand the success of my mine.

Difficulties accumulate. Popular opinion is against me for allowing Maachah to come out into these wilds; and I myself am doubting the wisdom of having brought her, for she is ailing under the heat and dryness of the place. More prospectors pour in every day. As well as the old-timers, there are crowds of down-and-outs hoping to strike it lucky. South Africa is suffering from a bad slump, and in certain parts one can see white men working along with blacks at road-making. When that happens things are bad indeed. The down-and-outs, of course, have nothing with them and the strain on my hospitality becomes still more hard to bear.

Then word comes to us from Jo'burg that our claim against the African Trust has been settled. We are asked to appear in Durban at a near date.

It is the final argument for abandoning our mining. Maachah is immensely relieved when I announce that we are going back to the world of the theater. I sell my various claims and make ready to depart. I leave behind a small town where I found a wilderness. Raau stays on and reaps a large benefit, for the new field turns out to be fairly successful.

We play for a week at the Criterion Theater in Durban, and are given the passage-money back to England which we have forfeited by instituting the law-suit against the Trust.

I sell Maachah's diamond to a licensed buyer for £7, and begin to wonder whether Raau was not being generous in his offer of £25. But there was something about the man . . . ! I'm glad I did not sell it to him.

*   *   *

Stretched across the deck are long ribbons of cloth two to three inches wide which are tied firmly to the rail. At the free ends a dozen flushed and eager women stand waiting for the signal to go, each with a pair of scissors in her hand. The signal is given.

The dozen start industriously cutting up the middles of the tapes. It is a famous deck-game. The winner is the lady who succeeds in cutting up the complete length of her tape and thus reaching the rail first. She must, however, cut the tape into two pieces only. If her scissors stray over the edge of one of the pieces and sever it, she is disqualified from the race.

There are, as usual on shipboard, large bets on the entrants. Most of the punters have put their money on competitors whom they have found out by divers means to be domestic women accustomed to making dresses and skilled in the expert use of scissors. Now the racers, urged on by the shouts of their backers, are snipping furiously as they advance toward the rail. Here and there one of them cuts one of her two halves of tape and is ignominiously sent off the field.

Two of the entrants have got a flying start. Already they are almost at the winning-post, while the rest of the field follow far behind. And now the race is over. The two leaders have romped home, and the result is given as a dead-heat. Of the joint winners, one is my partner, Maachah. The other is our ship's celebrity, Miss Binnie Hale.

Already fresh bets are being laid as to the result of the play-off between the two winners. The odds are on Binnie Hale, but I fancy Maachah. My instinct is right. In the second race Maachah wins decisively.

To many it seems strange that, out of all the entrants in the race, the winners should be the two women who are the least domesticated of the field. I should think it quite likely that neither of them could cut out a dress from a pattern with any success, as all the other entrants probably could, yet they have left the others standing in this game. The fact is that, both being stage-folk, they are accustomed to performing in public. The other ladies are nervous, but these two are cool as cucumbers. They have conquered the terrors of stage fright. The others have not.

*   *   *

With a penknife, I make a tiny fiddle just eight inches long. Used through a microphone it gives results which I am told are extraordinary. Almost my first time of playing it in public is at a function at the Belgian Embassy, at which Prince Arthur of Connaught is present.

After I have ended my recital, my partner takes the diminutive instrument round among the guests to let them see it. She hands it to Prince Arthur first. He smiles and asks:

"What am I supposed to say about this?"

"Well, sir, have you ever seen anything like it before?"

"Often, but they have always been several times the size."

"Don't you think it's remarkable then?"

He smiles again.

"I think it's so remarkable as to be almost incredible."

* * *

I am back in England after a long tour during which I have visited France, Spain, Hungary and Italy, ending up with an engagement at Shepheard's Hotel in Cairo. From Egypt I have brought back my customary collection of the native fauna. I have taken a house in Cornwall for a while, installed my collection, and settled down to a period of quiet. My dogs, who have accompanied me on part of the trip abroad, are installed meantime in a local church as quarantine. Why it should be a church I cannot tell, but can only assume that Cornwall is suffering from a religious slump.

The time comes for me to return to London, and I prepare to transport my collection. But one member of it is missing. A puff-adder cannot be found anywhere, and the only plausible explanation is that it has escaped from its home in the conservatory and made for the highways and byways. I have to leave Cornwall without it.

I wonder what has happened to my puff-adder. Is he still struggling to pick up meager sustenance amid the barren beauty of the Cornish scene; has some normal snake-detesting human smashed him to pulp with a walking-stick; or—worse still—has he fallen into the hands of a new master who does not understand him and treats him cruelly? If he is

being badly used wherever he is now, I only hope
that, during his brief spell of liberty, he put the fear
of death into a long succession of old ladies and
scared many a drunkard into repentance by appearing suddenly on the road.

*   *   *

Conceiving the idea for creating a new act for
the stage, I advertise for a girl-artiste able to play
a musical instrument, to be my partner in it, and ask
the applicants to appear at the flat which I have
already established as my headquarters in London.

In the morning of the appointed day I go out,
coming back at the hour set for the appointment. I
enter my room and find upwards of twenty girls
in it!

Momentarily I suffer a bad attack of stage fright.
I mumble and yammer foolishly, and at last summon
enough remnants of aplomb to suggest that I should
listen to each of them in turn. Feeling rather like a
bloated pantomime producer at an audition, I sit
back and listen as one after another plays for me.
What a pity it is, I think as I listen, that so many
talented young musicians should be looking for a
job. . . .

What a pity that I am forced to choose only one
from the crowd!

The last one plays, and I have still to choose.
They are all so good that I simply cannot pick out

one in particular. I sit in frustrated silence for a long time, and one of the girls says pleasantly:

"Well, do you mind telling us which of us are unlucky, because my mother's expecting me home for lunch?"

"I only wish I could take you all. You're all so good that I simply don't know which of you to take," I confessed.

"Why not take us all?" asks one.

"He'd need to start a band to do that," another retorts jokingly.

In an instant I realize that that idle remark provides the answer to the question. Why *not* start a ladies' band? I have certainly enough talent for one here. I get up from my chair and bow my defeat.

"Very well then. You win. I shall start a band."

And in this unpremeditated fashion is born my Ladies' Hussars Band. I select fifteen of the girls, but need a drummer. Maachah, although she has never played the drums before, practises hard and becomes amply competent to fill that breach. We get down to rehearsals with a will.

The Kit-Kat Club announces that it wishes to engage a band to play permanently there. I go to a theatrical costumier's and obtain a set of glittering uniforms for my girls. Along with a number of other bands, we present ourselves at the Kit-Kat for an audition. My girls perform like veterans, and we carry the day. It is a great occasion: we have got our first engagement!

XIX

WHAT IS A GYPSY?

ARE gypsies the children of a wild secret folk out of Egypt or India; wild and romantic; foreign and proud of their foreignness; jealously guarding their dark customs and esoteric tongue from the curiosity of the despised Gorgio; loving the open road and spurning the hearth; discussing any implication on the impregnable chastity of their women at the point of the knife?

That is what one might believe to be the truth about gypsies, if one had acquired one's knowledge of them out of Borrow and a regiment of later writers. That is, indeed, what one might believe who had acquired one's facts from gypsies themselves. For, after all, most gypsies depend for their livelihood upon the popular legends current about them. It is not much use claiming to tell the future if you are not a strange and secret person with strange and secret knowledge. And, if you are "interesting," you may be tolerated to camp on the property of the Lord of the Manor; whereas, if you are merely one of a gang of tramps, you are likely to be turned on your way with small ceremony.

Nearly all the popular legends referring to gypsies

273

center round their exclusiveness. Language, customs, and sundry strange powers are all supposed to be more or less secret. One reads of privileged Gorgios being "initiated" into the Brotherhood of the Black Tents, with strange rites, including much flourishing of knives and swearing of loyalty and "blood-brotherhood."

The truth is that gypsies have never been exclusive. On the contrary, forming as they do a community of the lowest and poorest, the people who are without property, they have consistently provided a haven for down-and-outs of any description. The broken soldier, the unlucky gambler, the discharged groom, the ex-convict—where could they find fellowship save among the broken folk like themselves? And, whether Gorgio or Romany, they found it with the gypsies, wandered the roads with them, lived with them, married them; and for the Gorgio vagrant of parts who joined the caravans, there was no need of "initiation."

Once it is accepted that the Romany folk are not exclusive, it is clear that this steady influx of Gorgios into the community must have been going on for generations. In consequence, even if there was originally a race out of Asia who wandered to the West and settled in Western countries but always remained apart and retained their purity of descent, the constant dilution of the pure stock by countless generations of Gorgios must have left hardly one person alive today who is a pure-blooded descendant of that original Asiatic race.

Moreover, the conviction that gypsies are a dark people as regards coloring is merely another fallacy. One finds Romanies of every coloring, even to red-haired people and platinum blondes. True, one does find a certain proportion of noticeably dark men and women amongst us, just as one finds such among more or less pure-blooded Anglo-Saxons; but it would be strange if one did not. What of our traditional old companions of the road—the old organ-grinders, invariably Italians; the bear-leaders, who were almost solely Asiatics or Levantines? Again assuming that gypsies are non-exclusive, we can explain away our darker element by these.

As regards the Romany language, I am ready to believe the learned men who say that it has its roots in India. But whether it came from there centuries ago, or merely during the last few generations, is not so clear. Just as soldiers brought back from the Great War their "napoo" and "san fairy ann," soldiers for generations back have been bringing back from India garbled versions of Indian words. One knows that not so very long ago many of these ex-soldiers came out of the army completely unequipped for civilian life and became tramps. To me it seems likely that a certain proportion of the words of Indian origin in Romany came from this source, for just as gypsies can understand the argot of professional tramps, so can the tramps understand much of the Romany language.

I do not suggest, of course, that all Romany words came from ex-soldiers from India. I merely point it out as something which philologists might take into consideration. And speaking of philologists, I was interested to hear one of these learned gentlemen tracing a word of ours, "grenadia," directly back to Sanskrit. I could have told him its true origin. In other days soldiers had a habit of buying things at fair-grounds and not paying for them, so certain of my own relatives would give each other warning when a purchaser was a soldier. To say it outright would not have done, so the word "grenadier" was commonly used, modifying itself in time to "grenadia."

No doubt all I have said about gypsies will be indignantly contested by those who believe the legends. It is not pleasant to have a romantic belief "debunked." All I ask is that the believers go to the nearest fair-ground and observe the van-dwellers; and, if they find the latter uniformly a bold, independent, dark-skinned, white-toothed, hot-blooded, secret, romantic community, I shall eat my words with gusto. But I fear they will be disappointed. If gypsies were the gypsies of legend in past centuries, all I can say is that "they ain't what they used to be." Nowadays one does not even need to live in a van or tent to qualify as one of the brotherhood; let him merely tell fortunes and sell trinkets at fairs, and he is a gypsy.

For all that I have said of an incredulous nature, I nevertheless have my own beliefs. I believe, for instance, that of the blood in my veins a great proportion is of the authentic ancient race. Certainly my appearance suggests it, and, although some problematical Assyrian ancestor may account for my peculiar physical characteristics, I know that for three or four generations back at least my forebears have been consistently black-haired and swarthy, with strange long faces; the reason for which, I like to think, is that the line of Prastermengros from whom I am sprung were one of the few Romany castes to own any real pride of race. If any were exclusive, they were; and, living well upon the road as they did, they had less temptation than other vagabonds to leave the road for the hearthside.

That my blood is not altogether pure, however, I know, for my great-great-grandfather married a woman of the Gorgios and took her to live with him among the Prastermengros on the roads. This Gorgio woman was a daughter of a farmer named Miles of Dumplin Green farm in Norfolk, and it was on this farm that George Borrow was born. There is a story in my family to the effect that this ancestor of mine was the original from which the "Petulengro" in Borrow's *Lavengro* was drawn; so that it was not altogether at random that I assumed the name "Petulengro" for professional purposes many years ago.

Perhaps, after all, my urge to wander is generated by the genuine gypsy blood in me. Perhaps conversely the sedentary tendencies of present-day gypsies is due simply to the fact that they are not true gypsies at all. Perhaps, when my fiddling days are done and all the members of my Ladies' Hussars Band have flitted from me, I shall take to the road again. Perhaps Borrow, that dramatizer of the gypsy and fairy-godmother of all cheap-jacks and rogues, would find something queer and alien in me that he found in my great-great-grandfather. Perhaps there is something in the gypsy legend after all?